Embedded Systems Architecture for Agile Development

A Layers-Based Model

Mohsen Mirtalebi

Apress®

Embedded Systems Architecture for Agile Development: A Layers-Based Model

Mohsen Mirtalebi
Indianapolis, Indiana, USA

ISBN-13 (pbk): 978-1-4842-3050-3   ISBN-13 (electronic): 978-1-4842-3051-0
https://doi.org/10.1007/978-1-4842-3051-0

Library of Congress Control Number: 2017957715

Cover image by Freepik (www.freepik.com)

Managing Director: Welmoed Spahr
Editorial Director: Todd Green
Acquisitions Editor: Susan McDermott
Development Editor: Laura Berendson
Technical Reviewer: Amir Shahirinia
Coordinating Editor: Rita Fernando
Copy Editor: Karen Jameson

Distributed to the book trade worldwide by Springer Science+Business Media New York, 233 Spring Street, 6th Floor, New York, NY 10013. Phone 1-800-SPRINGER, fax (201) 348-4505, e-mail orders-ny@springer-sbm.com, or visit www.springeronline.com. Apress Media, LLC is a California LLC and the sole member (owner) is Springer Science + Business Media Finance Inc (SSBM Finance Inc). SSBM Finance Inc is a **Delaware** corporation.

For information on translations, please e-mail rights@apress.com, or visit http://www.apress.com/rights-permissions.

Apress titles may be purchased in bulk for academic, corporate, or promotional use. eBook versions and licenses are also available for most titles. For more information, reference our Print and eBook Bulk Sales web page at http://www.apress.com/bulk-sales.

Any source code or other supplementary material referenced by the author in this book is available to readers on GitHub via the books product page, located at www.apress.com/9781484230503. For more detailed information, please visit http://www.apress.com/source-code.

*To my parents who put up with my handyman
projects since age four when I was first
electrocuted attempting to fix the TV. To my son
who has patiently learned that I only answer the
calls after the sixth attempt. This is why I was slow.*

Table of Contents

About the Author xi

About the Technical Reviewer xiii

Introduction xv

Chapter 1: The History of Layers Architecture................................... 1

The New and the Old.. 4

Clash of Cultures.. 5

Clash of Thoughts 5

Projects and Processes... 6

Products and People 6

Product Software 7

Embedded Systems 7

Process Bottlenecks 8

Intelligent Product Development... 8

Architecture in the Construction Industry 9

Land Survey Drawings.. 10

Architectural Drawings 12

Drawing's Reusability, Maintainability, Readability, and Scalability............ 22

Making Buildings versus Making PCBs... 24

Summary... 25

Chapter 2: Project Management Methods 27

The Basics... 28

Project Management Using Critical Path Methods (CPM) 28

What Is CPM? 29

Creating a Robust Gantt Chart 29

Project Management Using Agile Methods 36

    What Does Agile Mean? 37

    The Ideal Scrum 37

Collaborative Product Development (CPD) 43

    Tasks, Deliverables, and Decisions 44

Software and Project Management 47

    Software Layers 47

    Software Development Process 49

    Software Reusability, Maintainability, Readability, and Scalability 51

    Software throughout CPD Process 52

    V-Model (Software Life Cycle) 53

Design for Manufacturing (DFM) 54

Modeling Languages and Agile 56

    Unified Modeling Language (UML) 56

    Model-Based Design (MBD) 56

Summary 57

Bibliography 59

Chapter 3: Convergence of Management and Architecture **61**

Convergence of Management and Architecture 62

    A Requirement Model 63

Creating Requirements 70

    Every Problem Is a Communication Problem 70

    Marketing Requirements Document (MRD) 74

    Conceptual Design 75

    Architecture Design 82

    Module Design 83

    Component Design and Product Breakdown Structure (PBS) 86

Summary 89

Bibliography 90

Chapter 4: Requirements Model **91**

Process and Control Requirements Model 91

    Context Diagrams 92

    Flow Diagrams 95

    Process and Control Specification (PSPEC, CSPEC) 97

    The Requirements Dictionary 99

    Timing Specifications 100

    A Note on Requirements Model 101

Structured Scrum 104

    Simplified V-Model 104

    PBS Development 114

    A Different Approach in Design 116

    Processing the External Data 118

    Bringing It All Together 120

    Utilizing MBD Tools for PBS 122

Summary 122

Bibliography 123

Chapter 5: Problem Statement **125**

Understanding the Problem 125

Requirements Model 126

    Data Context and Control Context Diagrams (DCD, CCD) 127

    Data Flow and Control Flow Diagrams (DFD, CFD) 129

    PSPEC and CSPEC 135

    Timing Specification 137

    Requirements Dictionary 138

    Architectural Model 139

Summary 140

Bibliography 141

Chapter 6: Process Architecture...**143**

   Proof of Concept 145

      Hardware Recycling...147

      Software Recycling..148

      Method Recycling...148

      Team Dynamics in Concept Release..................................148

      Scrum and the Concept Release 150

   Architecture and Planning..153

      Hardware Recycling...154

      Software Recycling..154

      Method Recycling...155

      Team Dynamics 155

   Modules and Components Releases 155

   The Final Release..157

      Departing from CPD and Landing on Structured Scrum 157

   Smoke Test...159

   Agile Testing...160

   Summary...160

Chapter 7: Layers Model **163**

   What Is a Model? 163

   Process and Product Models 164

      Product's Process Model...166

      Development Process Model 169

   MBD Tools 172

   MBD Utilization Steps...173

   Layer Model and MBD 174

   MBD's Build Process 177

   MBD in Layers Model 179

   MBD Platforms 181

   Summary...182

   Bibliography 182

Chapter 8: MBD and Requirements Model **183**

Product Model 186

MBD and Process Model 195

    Timing Specifications 196

    Requirements Dictionary 198

    Real-Time Operating Systems 199

    Database Architecture 200

    Verification and Validation (V&V) 201

    Continuous Integration 203

    Smoke Test 203

    Manufacturing Tests 204

    Diagnostics 204

Summary 205

Index **207**

About the Author

 **Mohsen Mirtalebi** is a specialist in diagnostics software with Cummins Inc., a global power leader that designs, manufactures, sells, and services diesel and alternative fuel engines as well as related components and technologies. He has more than 10 years of experience in the engineering field. At Cummins, Mohsen leads a team of engineers, where he oversees the software quality meeting regulatory requirements by utilizing various data analysis tools, controls software reviews, as well as Agile and project management tools. Previously he worked for Rockwell Automation as a control firmware engineer, responsible for control algorithm design and implementation for motor drives utilizing MBD, and real-time operating systems. He has held other hardware/software positions at Danfoss, Emerson Process Management, and more. Computer skills include being a certified user of Matlab/Simulink, LabView/TestStand and Texas Instrument DSC/DSP products specializing in motion devices. Mohsen has a MS in Electrical Engineering with an emphasis on power electronics control and HIL/SIL/MIL. He has been a member of IEEE for 10 years. He is an advocate of STEM and has coached many robotics teams in grade schools.

About the Technical Reviewer

Dr. Amir Shahirinia is an Assistant Professor of the Department of Electrical and Computer Engineering at the University of the District of Columbia, Washington, DC. He received BS and MS degrees from K.N.Toosi University of Techology, Tehran, Iran, and a PhD from University of Wisconsin-Milwaukee in Electrical Engineering. He also performed postdoctoral research in the Power Electronics group at Rockwell Automation (Allen Bradly) from 2013–2015. Dr. Shahirinia is the director of Center of Excellence for Renewable Energy (CERE) at UDC. Dr. Shahirinia's research interests encompass the areas of power systems, smart grids, power electronics, and control and ranges from optimal planning of renewable energy grid integration systems (REGIS), optimal operations of REGIS, modeling and intelligent real-time control of REGIS, Bayesian statistical analysis and predictive modeling of REGIS, to power electronics and motor drives.

Introduction

What do onions and software have in common? Apparently there is nothing in common between them, but how many things around us are inspired by nature? Years ago I was hired by a high-tech company for what was, I thought at the time, one of the coolest products. Here I was in a small manufacturing company with a high innovative spirit but not part of a highly meaningful organization. For a duration of two and half months I had nothing to do but to get myself familiarized with the product, and I loved it. So as a free agent I started roaming around every corner of the company, visiting many departments from quality control to hardware, manufacturing, program management, and even product returns.

The result of two and half months of my spiritual journey into the deep belly of the product was to discover that there were numerous holes in our development process of which many were software related. Since our product target and host software were closely coupled, which were also utilized internally for various applications such as product calibration and tests, I came up with a 30-page report including some recommendations to improve the quality of the software architecture on both ends: target and host software. I thought it could be cost effective to enhance the existing architecture rather than investing in a new platform. Additionally, there were some serious security concerns. Our OEM customers were using the same host software, and the chances of breaching the engineering tier was high. Perhaps when our OEM customer was talking to us, we didn't do a good job of listening; and now they had to take the matter into their own capable hands to tweak some product configuration parameters for us.

On that account, listening to the customer's voice is essential. Either we choose to listen to them when we are developing the requirements or were forced to do so when the hammer comes down on us through the product return doors. Although we might think the product research and returns are two different departments, in fact they are the same with a minor difference. These two departments fall on the two ends of product development process, but in both, people get into the same type of cause-and-effect cycles. The difference falls into the chronology of the product issues.

A new anomaly in returns most likely is an old known one in research. The reason some people might think it is a new problem is because the problem was either overlooked, forgotten, or currently being worked on – in secrets without notifying other internal departments. So if there was a way we could capture this wealth of knowledge that we've tirelessly gained during product R&D, then there is a very good chance we can better manage them downstream. This is called transparency.

In another example with a different manufacturer, I observed that the products of a well-known test and measurement vendor were extensively used in the R&D department. Although the manufacturing was not using the same type of test tools, but their test routines were basically the same only designed to be more subjective and shorter in duration. Then I thought if I could convert the tools in manufacturing to be matched with R&D tools, I could recycle research software programs for manufacturing uses. So that was exactly what I did. The result was a seamless path between development and manufacturing that not only unified the tools but also the languages these two very different departments were speaking. This was more than creating a scalable test process; it was about creating a freeway of knowledge – the very knowledge that distinguishes one product, one company, one country from another.

Coming back to my 30-page report, I received the worst possible review. "Huh?!" was the only reply I got from the executive management. I don't blame them. If anyone else was in their shoes, reading a technical report that compares a software to an onion, you could most likely have the same reaction. So why on earth did I make this comparison?

It's simple, because onions do not rot in a way other perishable produce do. The progress of decay in an onion is in layers. If the outside layers get infected by bacteria, the inner layers would be still intact. This is because each layer is carefully isolated and independent from another layer. So if you haven't guessed it by now, I had proposed a new software architecture based on targeted functional layers specific for different applications.

You might ask now how the Layers architecture works? The concept of layers is to reduce dependencies between various engineering disciplines involved in product development while keeping the functionality of the software intact. Layers also help to break the development constraints in a multiplatform product consisting of hardware and software. As we know, hardware and software follow their own life cycle at their own pace. Often we see that either the hardware gets a head start while software waits for the hardware development to complete, or often the software becomes much more complex than its own hardware platform. In either case, software is always late, incomplete, and buggy. Unfortunately this is the case in every embedded systems market that makes the software the bottleneck in our product development processes.

The first golden rule of removing the bottlenecks is to remove dependencies. This is not 20 years ago when we didn't have tools to do hardware in the loop (HIL), software in the loop (SIL), or model in the loop (MIL) simulations. Back then we didn't have evaluation boards handy for every product. We can now simulate the entire product no matter how complex its functionality is. However, you might ask, we have the tools but why aren't our processes still not as efficient? It's because the tools can't think. What we need is a trusted process that would enable us to organize our thoughts systematically and across various engineering disciplines. Layers is a work frame that will enable us to architect our products before they are even formed into a meaningful concepts. It is an organic process solely based on our understanding of our own customer's requirements. It is organic because it is formed based on your application, product, organization, and company's culture. Once we inputted and analyzed the customer's voice, then the developers and the tools can take over and breathe through the development process – from research, to design, to manufacturing, deployment, and beyond.

Nevertheless, this is not the end of the story: there are still various other bottlenecks in the development. Testing is one of those. Product testing is one of the lengthiest and possibly the single most expensive item in the development. In addition, various engineering departments design and perform their own engineering/manufacturing tests independently from one another and often unknowingly overlap in test scopes. Since Layers emphasizes independence, the chances of redundancy would increase even more. However if a common product integration tool is used across all the development, this common language would make the redundancies evident to the designers; therefore they can address it beforehand. But this is not enough because the ultimate goal is to remove lengthy and expensive redundancies in the test in order to make our processes lean.

To create lean processes you can't just jump into buying fancy tools yet, unless you'd like to add to your collection of very expensive dust collectors. We need an active product architecture that is designed based on the customer's specific needs. With the help of the Requirements Model and Model-Based Design tools, creating and maintaining an active product architecture is easier than ever. Furthermore, these tools will enable the development team, from research to manufacturing, to cut back on the amount of documentations without compromising the integrity of the design. For the people who are worried about government regulations and scrutiny of its various branches such as DOD, FDA, DOT, DOE, EPA, ARB, etc., this would provide a documentation system with a robust traceability feature for your design.

Although the "onion" architecture belonged to that particular company facing a specific security problem, the idea of layers can well be expanded into any existing development whether in software, hardware, or a mixture of both, especially in embedded systems. Each department only needs a portion of this software while still receiving the majority of product knowledge. The idea of layers will provide a solution to unify the different languages that now exist in each development segment. It reduces the rework and the time to market, and most importantly saves money, which in return enables the manufacturers to stay competitive not only locally but globally. The macroeconomic impact of deploying intelligent development and product architecture such as Layers would not be dismissive. It is now time to turn away from looking at software as a commodity and see it as a conduit in which knowledge flows.

Finally, by removing the constraints in our development processes, we would be able to implement one Agile framework for development for both hardware and software rather than having a hodgepodge of traditional V-Model or Water Fall in software and ancient phase-gate (CPD)/CPM systems for our hardware. Nevertheless, you still can represent your progress in a phase-gate approach if you choose to, but the development team won't be bugged down by it as they will follow the Agile approach. All these would empower the development team who is doing the bulk of the work to synchronize their paces across the board while keeping a desirable cadence to deliver incremental values to the customers.

CHAPTER 1

The History of Layers Architecture

What does developing a real-time system project have in common with a construction project, from the project management perspective? Can we develop and manage both projects with the same methodologies and tools? Some of you might think from a project management standpoint, developing real-time or embedded systems should not resemble developing a construction project. Although both might look similar organizationally and share the same types of resources such as time, money, and people; however, the fact that software has become an integral part of embedded systems will significantly differentiate these two projects from each other. Now, this important question arises: why is it that in many companies, both developments are called projects and use the same project management tools? The answer to this question will go beyond the boundaries of what the science of management can offer. This is because the sciences involved with developing real-time systems are very new and are in a constant state of change. Therefore the word "project" might carry a misleading connotation when it's used for developing embedded systems. But this misconception has deeper roots than one might think. We all have seen many leaders in the embedded systems industry still utilize the same tools and methods that a construction company uses in developing their projects.

Nevertheless there are very valuable lessons in studying the construction projects, not in the management methods that have been used for years but in their own schools of thought. The construction industry has evolved through their thousands of years of history. All in all, the traditional management tools can work for real-time systems projects but in no way can one call this type of project management efficient for developing mid- to large-size embedded systems. Through reading this book you will realize how developing embedded systems are fundamentally different from any other types of projects. To start off, let's avoid the use of the term "project" temporarily as it

© Mohsen Mirtalebi 2017
M. Mirtalebi, *Embedded Systems Architecture for Agile Development*,
https://doi.org/10.1007/978-1-4842-3051-0_1

might misleadingly imply only a process. An embedded system development is not just a process, it is a product integrated into a process. Although you might say a physical building is considered a product but it is not, because it lacks manufacturing of the same building in a volume of thousands of identical copies. Since a building is not a product, therefore, the term "project" shouldn't apply to embedded systems. If you want, you can, but keep in mind, our embedded system development project implies the process and product.

The fact that there will be thousands of copies of what you are making in the market makes the concept of efficiency of grave importance. An efficient development method results in an efficient product, and this translates directly to waste elimination, which creates direct economic impacts on both our company and customers through our process and products respectively. If we reduce the cost of development, our product would become cost effective and more competitive in pricing. In return it will bring a considerable amount of saving of costs to our customers. Combine efficiency and the astronomical numbers of embedded systems used currently across the globe, and we will come to the realization that the efficiency we intend to create will propagate to the furthest corner of the earth. Now this is a true green process. So forget not about the green products, but instead imagine your product will be the greenest of all. However, for some reasons, the idea of green in the industry has been slowly becoming a concept confined only to some promotional tools for marketing biodegradable materials in products or environmentally compliant methods such as ISO14000.

Although the recent waves of the green movement in the waste management and manufacturing process improvements are very good starting points for creating efficient systems, the bulk of waste in resources happens during development of products of any sorts. It is ironic that the term "green," which would imply efficient should result in lower costs; but rather it imposes additional compliance regulations by which the manufacturers must assign budgets to maintain. This will result in higher developmental costs and longer product time to market, which consequently results in higher product prices defeating the purpose of being green. As we can see, a true green process results in better economic impacts such as a lower finished cost of the product without compromising the quality of the product. Therefore our concept of green runs a bit deeper, and it starts from where the first idea of a product sparks; however, it doesn't stop there and it continues to bear fruit while it runs its entire course of product life cycle. The Agile method of development is one way to reduce the waste since these methodologies were initially created to specifically target waste; however there are two shortcomings in these frameworks. One is that most Agile methods are optimized for software products, not embedded systems that are comprised of both software and hardware. Also, embedded systems are produced in order to carry out critical applications where general purpose computers are not to be trusted to perform the tasks; therefore saving costs is not the main objective of creating these systems.

In other words, most real-time systems are mainly designed to carry out control functions with critical applications. The Agile methods give waste elimination the highest priority, which could make us happy about the efficiency portion, but they fail to put enough emphasis on the robustness of the product. A good example of this is the Microsoft products that are developed through Agile methods. Their numerous after-release software patches and their daily software updates are evident that robustness is not high on their list. We are not to blame one product over its lack of quality. What we want to say is that, when there is not enough emphasis on one aspect of product or there is so much of it on another aspect, people who follow those methods blindly might not be able to put things in perspective. In addition, since in the span of development time and also product life cycle the technology and hardware components can change, it is very important to plan carefully ahead. While an Agile method empowers the project to deal with short-term changes, it might make it easier for its followers to abandon long-term plans for the product. The real consequence of this approach is that the importance of architecture in product development will be devalued. As you can see later, the product architecture plays a vital role in developing the embedded systems.

A project manager, in any type of project, from construction to hi-tech needs to put several hats on during the life of the project. In a real-time system development project, a manager needs to interface with different stakeholders and internal and external customers at different phases of a project and needs to follow various life cycles including project, product, and software life cycles. However, a project manager is hardly a product architect. This is because most project managers are trained and skillful in the art of management rather than designing a real-time system. This book is intended to find the common aspects of various life cycles and introduce an inclusive methodology that would cover them all under one umbrella with an emphasis on the necessary amount of documentation. We are hoping that by the end by reading this book, if not anything, at least your outlook will change toward real-time systems development.

Furthermore, this book is for the embedded system project architects who are aware of steps involving developing a real-time system and not just the project. The detail of how to become aware of the design steps is through systematic use of a tool called the requirement model. This new addition to what Agile methods seem to be lacking will empower the project architects to create a robust architecture that would very well address the criticality of a real-time system development while creating an efficient process and product. The advantage of following an Agile method will break the never-ending cycle of analysis-paralysis that most classical product development methods suffer from. Nevertheless, we all know that the classical methods are the foundation of the new methods; therefore, the ideas discussed here might be new but backward compatible and are absolutely true to the traditional methods, especially the CPD framework. Nevertheless, this book will not discuss the details of any design standards; software and hardware testing methods such as white box, black box, or any hardware development phase such as hardware alpha and beta prototyping; and manufacturing bottlenecks such as functional and end-of-the line testing, but it will show you how to utilize these methods and tools when you get to the different phases of development.

Nevertheless, if we look at the nature, there is a great lesson in it, that anything and everything in nature happens for a reason. There is no beauty for the sake of only beauty. Any vibrant or dull color and exotic or subtle shape carries a reason. It is useless to talk about team structure and function if we don't know the mission. A mission creates a structure and a structure delivers a function. As Louise Henry Sullivan, the father of skyscrapers and the founder of the school of organic architecture said, "Form Follows Function." This book is to show you how to build your processes around the product.

The New and the Old

If you are coming from an Industrial Engineering background, you know that a simple Gantt chart would never satisfy you if you are planning a project. This is because you believe a project must have a baseline. But why don't most project managers create project baselines? It is because it's a tedious job as you have to break down the project to the units of work per person, which are called tasks, then you have to go on to load all the tasks with resources that they are required to have their own work calendars. Finally you have to apply the logical and temporal constraints to see how the tasks line up, and at the end you have to level the resources by sliding the tasks in the schedule. Therefore, creating a simple Gantt chart by no means is project planning and control. Years later when I changed gears in my career and became an electrical engineer, to my astonishment I saw the embedded system development projects were managed the same way as a construction project was managed.

However, considering the short history of electronics, software, and computer engineering relative to other branches of engineering such as mechanical, chemical, and civil, these new disciplines are still at their infancy stage with respect to work standardization and offering best practices. Nevertheless, our modern manufacturing and the backbone of our industries are built on the foundation of these new branches of engineering. So the storyline goes like this: there are three young sheriffs in our town and they are clueless.

Clash of Cultures

In every traditional development project there are two types of people. People who know the product and people who know the project and hardly enough people who know the product and project at the same time. People who know the product can tell you very well what the product is comprised of. They can identify the sub-assemblies, modules, and components; and they can break down the product into various functions. People who know the project can arrange development and manufacturing work in such way that product or concepts would come to life through the path of the least resistance. However, both groups of people have one thing in common: they are concerned about the constraints. Product-oriented crowds want to establish constraints and project-oriented individuals want to avoid them. This brings up a very interesting phenomenon in product development and manufacturing: the clash of cultures.

Clash of Thoughts

By definition, a project is a unique set of activities that a distinctive team of people carry out only once. On the other hand, a process is what a fixed number of people do routinely. With respect to constraints, projects want to remove the constraints and processes want to solidify them. In classical project planning, the project manager starts drafting the project with no constraints in mind, with the sort of 9-women-giving-birth-to-a-child-in-a-month mentality. Therefore, ideally all project activities start at the same time and continue concurrently. Consequently, the project managers don't want any resource, material, and budget constraints. However, in an engineering process everything is diagonally opposing this view. Engineers, for example, want design reviews before approvals, prototypes before releases, and so forth. This brings us to another fundamental difference between processes and projects; let's call it the clash of school of thoughts.

Projects and Processes

By calling a product development, which inherently has a procedural nature, a project, you bound yourself, your team, and your company to utilize project planning and control methods and tools instead of utilizing methods and tools that were specific to the processes. This is contradictory to the nature of product development, because a product development is much closer in nature to manufacturing, which is also process based, than being a project in its classical form. Let's remember that the most powerful modern product development methodologies such as Lean and Agile come from manufacturing environments but in contrast, the project management methods and tools are originated from the non-manufacturing environments.

Let's assume your company manufactures switching power supplies in various sizes for different applications. Your company has two main lines of products, a fixed line with the highest volume of production; and a custom line that is low in volume but for special applications. You, as an owner, decide to call these two product lines differently. You call the more established product line a process and the custom line or any new product development, a project. In the best case, you decide to use a common pool of resources to support both lines; otherwise you have no option but to have two parallel teams with the same skill sets to work on two different lines. As long as you are using the same resources in the common pool to support and also develop products, you have created a very inefficient system with two very different product visions, project vs. process. But the worst case is when you use two different teams for these two different lines, and then you lose valuable product knowledge in transition from one team to another. In both cases your system has become highly inefficient.

Products and People

A product is nothing more than a collection of constraints that have been materialized. The size, value, scope, and functionality of a product are predefined from day one of its inception. The moment you envision a product in your mind you have constrained it. Consequently the product developers are people who are aware of these constraints and work around or with them to conceptualize the product. Let's say you start a new "project" and invite numerous subject-matter experts into the development team. Let's assume you invited Matt, an expert in power electronics hardware design, to the team.

He's been doing this for the last 15 years. To him, project x, y, and z don't mean much. All he cares about is to design a robust hardware that meets all the constraints or in better words all the requirements of any particular "project."

Product Software

Now the big question is where the software development falls into product development as a whole? Software is becoming a very integral part of our lives and it is growing fast in complexity, which is accepting a bigger portion of the product. The traditional software development methods and life cycles such as V-Model, waterfall, and so forth are project-based methods, because the hallmark of a project is that it has a distinctive start, an end, and some transitional stages in between. The reason V-Model and other software life cycles are so popular now in software development is because when software needed development methods, the only trusted methods available all had roots in project-based methodologies. Software science took off so fast that it left the method thinkers in the dust, giving no advance warning to them to come up with standards and established methods. But now we are at a different juncture of time where we have process-based methodologies such as Lean and Agile, which are gaining tremendous grounds in the industry. This is good news for the software industry but not good enough for the embedded systems.

Embedded Systems

These systems are neither purely hardware nor software but a combination of both. As a matter of fact, the software takes a different name in these systems, called firmware, emphasizing how firmly software is tied to the hardware. The fundamental problem that lays down in the nature of embedded systems is originated from how differently hardware and software are viewed from the developmental standpoint. By adopting two different methods in developing hardware and software separately, we create the clashes of thoughts and cultures resulting in enormous challenges in embedded systems development as how to synchronize the paces of development in software and hardware to minimize the development losses.

In an attempt to overcome this challenge, some cutting-edge industry leaders have decided to adopt two different approaches for hardware and software separately. Process-based methodologies are chosen for the firmware and project-based methods are chosen for their hardware development. But this, in no way, will help to resolve the initial issue. You still have two different mythologies under one roof for one product while creating additional problems with respect to the clashes of cultures and thoughts. Let's find out what's the root cause of this synchronization problem? To answer this we should look at what the bottlenecks are in the development of the embedded systems.

Process Bottlenecks

In my previous writings, I pointed out two major bottlenecks, firmware latencies, and test applications. For the embedded systems development, these two are the two sides of the same coin. The test bottleneck would be the real issue and the firmware bottleneck would be a consequential one. In other words, firmware development for an embedded system wouldn't cause any bottleneck if the hardware platform was readily available. But to develop the hardware we need firmware. To resolve this situation some people resort to developing their hardware beforehand to give the firmware a head start prior to the "project's" formal kickoff. But that will make your entire product development gravely inefficient, which not only increases the final cost of the product but also lowers the product quality.

The solution might be to utilize any of the in-the-loop methods such as Model in the Loop, Software in the Loop, and Hardware in the Loop, intelligently. We know that the in-the-loop methods have been utilized in the industry for a long time, but why there is still so much waste in our systems? This is because we don't know when exactly to deploy these tools. We have no plan and no road maps as how to resolve the bottleneck issues.

Intelligent Product Development

As we discussed before we should avoid managing our Hi-Tech developmental process like a construction project. But there is one thing we can learn from construction projects: no one in a construction project starts the project until every participating team is aware of the building or site architecture. You might think there are still a lot of embedded systems manufacturers who just do that. That's correct, but soon after the product architecture is in place, the product hardware and software take their own development paths only to synch by enforcing "project" management tools. An active product architecture would give us a road map on when to deploy our synchronization tools.

Architecture in the Construction Industry

The oldest profession in the world's history (although some might dispute this) is civil engineering. Looking at some examples of how civil engineering has evolved might be beneficial to one of the newest professions in the world, computer engineering. By looking at the time line of civil engineering, we believe that the materials, methods, and tools in construction engineering have not changed drastically. We can see the use of rocks, metals, concrete, and so on from a few thousand years ago until now. Although there have been many breakthroughs in the sciences involved in civil engineering in terms of tools, methods, and materials, since the evolution of this profession has been so gradual, it has provided the engineers enough adaptation time to vigorously test various ways of applying them.

For example, Persians used mud and hay as reinforced building materials to strengthen their buildings. Later the idea of reinforced building material such as concrete was used by Sullivan in the Auditorium building in Chicago. It reduced the massive weight of the buildings, allowing the building to go higher, providing them with more rooms inside and larger windows outside. He also invented reinforced concrete for the first time in the world that revolutionized the construction industry. From reinforced mud to reinforced concrete, there is a timespan of a few thousand years. What it means is that there has been a long period of adaptation time that allowed the civil engineers to get acquainted with the materials and their applications. But if we look carefully, the basics of making buildings have stayed the same for quite a long time. This has allowed the civil engineers and architects to polish their methods of engineering to perfection.

In contrast, the construction material in electrical engineering has evolved drastically within the last few decades. Although the base material of a building and a microprocessor chip is comprised of the same silicon element, there is a lot more complexity in application of this element in a silicon chip than, for example, in a floor tile made of ceramic. Going back to civil engineering, one of the tools engineers invented that is widely used today, even in other engineering disciplines and that was pioneered thousands of years ago, is the architectural drawing. These drawings have been utilized as the most effective tool to communicate with various trade professionals from the time of pyramids to the time of skyscrapers.

Land Survey Drawings

One of the first tasks in developing a new construction project is to identify the building site relative to its surrounding. In modern buildings the location of the construction site is marked through the use of cameras equipped with GPS with respect to the absolute coordinates. The survey drawing provides several advantages; it not only marks the building location, it also identifies the residents' access to the building as well as identifying the building's access to the city utility lines and in general its surrounding world. Figure 1-1 shows the topographical view of the construction site and the location of a residential building. The shape in bold in the middle is the location of the future building site, and the contour lines identify the shape of a landmark with a different elevation, perhaps marking a hillside. On the top of the figure you can see the access road to the site. Also the prospective building is surrounded by vegetation.

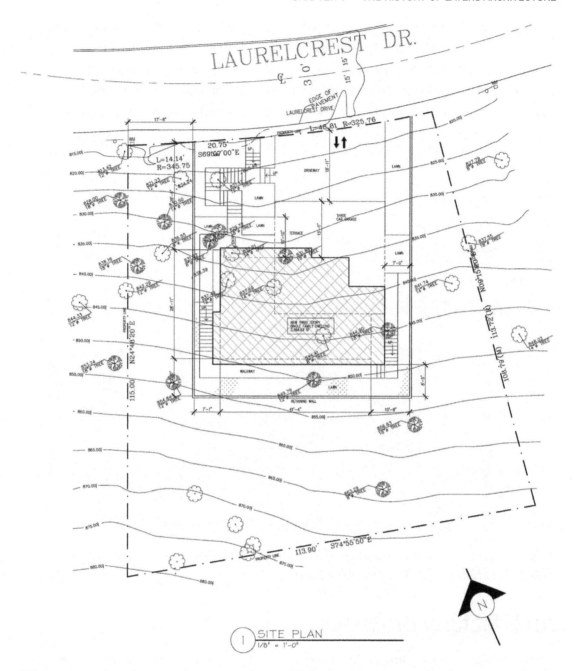

Figure 1-1. *Land surveying map of a candidate construction site (Courtesy of Afshin Kianpour)*

In Figure 1-2, you can see the enlarged portion of Figure 1-1. All the main access to the building from the outside world is meticulously designed from the stairways to lawns, driveway to the three-car garage, and the exact locations of each tree. In an analogy to an embedded system, this is the first step of realizing a customer's requirements in terms of a well-defined system with bounded inputs and outputs (BIBO).

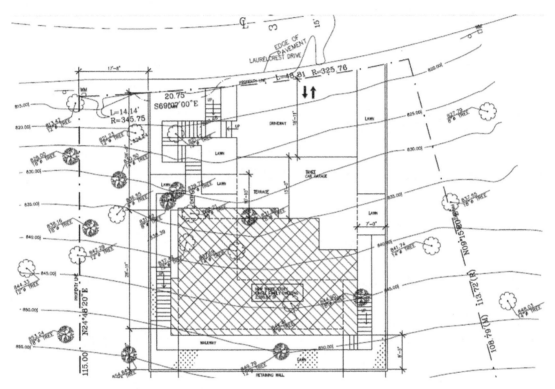

Figure 1-2. *Land surveying map of a candidate construction site (details of Figure 1-1) (Courtesy of Afshin Kianpour)*

Architectural Drawings

The next step in the long line of the civil engineering documentation process is the architectural drawing. Please note the architectural drawings are strictly hierarchical in nature and follow a top-down approach. They start from the perimeter of the building and then slowly move into the inside of the building explaining every detail, from material and tool specifications to showing access to a city's utilities in every room. To avoid crowding the drawings the information is categorized to a different level of abstraction. The principals are explained first then if it deemed necessary, more details would follow. In an architectural drawing every line of text carries critical information. In Figure 1-3 a plot plan of the building shows the building's perimeter, the main structure, and dimensions. The drawing shows the top view of the future building.

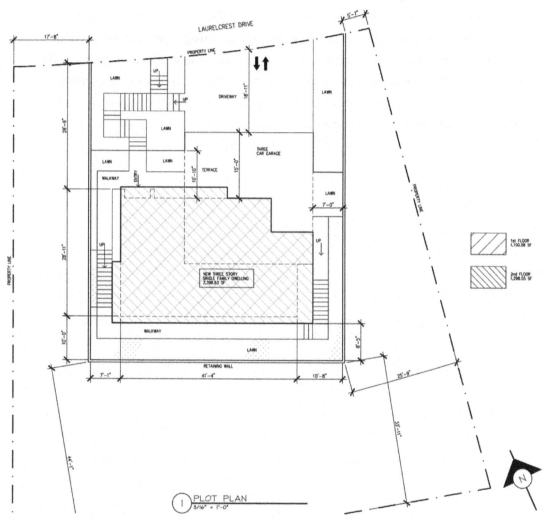

Figure 1-3. *Plot plan of a future building (Courtesy of Afshin Kianpour)*

A plot plan is to show the main modules of the building giving an overview of what comes next. In embedded systems this is called system specifications where the inputs, outputs, user interfaces, and main system functionality are defined in a very abstract fashion. The system spec is meant to unify the language of customer with the designers, creating a common language between them.

Since this is a three-story building the next three figures, Figures 1-4, 1-5, and 1-6, show the architectural details of these floors from garage level to the third floor level respectively. As you can see there is a massive amount of information packed on these sheets. All the measurements and locations for the walls, windows, columns, and stairways along references to other drawings and site designation for each room are clearly marked. For example by a quick inspection one can realize there is another drawing regarding the cross-sectional view of the building.

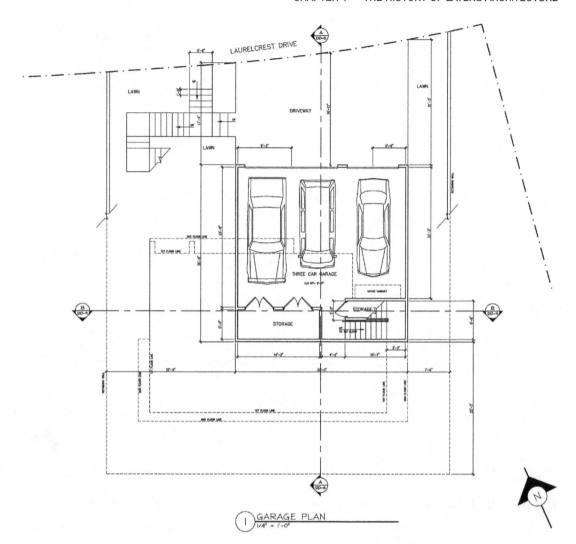

Figure 1-4. *Garage floor architectural drawing (Courtesy of Afshin Kianpour)*

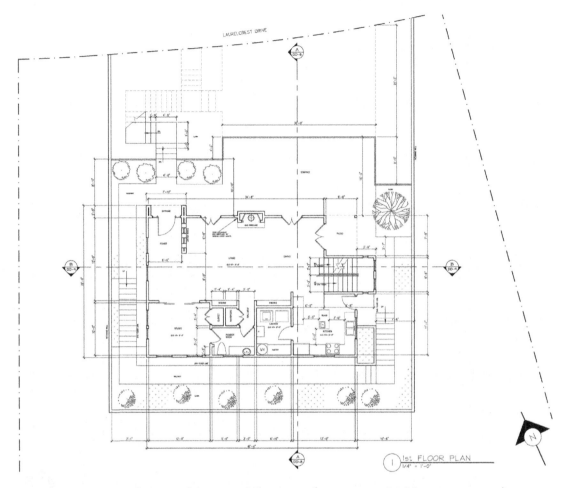

Figure 1-5. *First floor architectural drawing (Courtesy of Afshin Kianpour)*

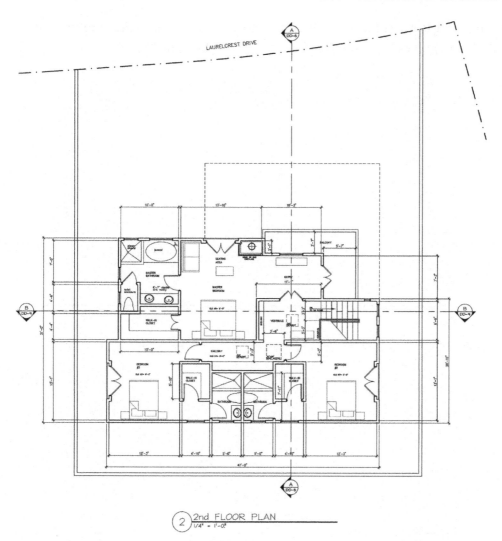

Figure 1-6. *Second floor architectural drawing (Courtesy of Afshin Kianpour)*

Since a building is a 3D object, to better help visualize it, the designers present the design with the building side views. Figures 1-7 and 1-8 illustrate that.

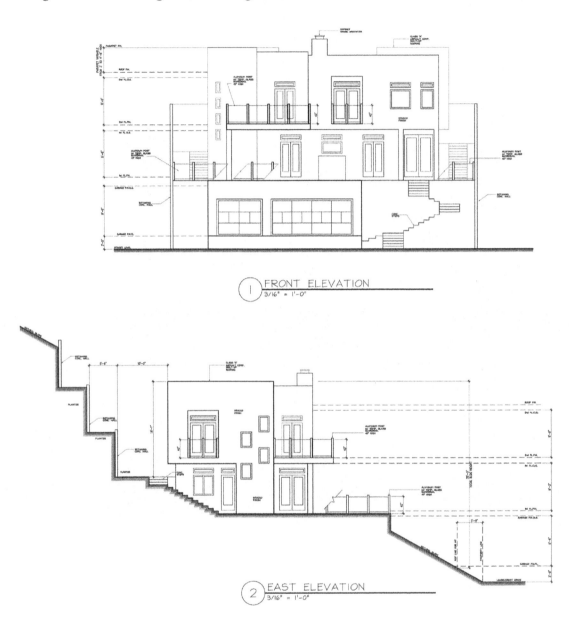

Figure 1-7. *Front and east elevation of the building (Courtesy of Afshin Kianpour)*

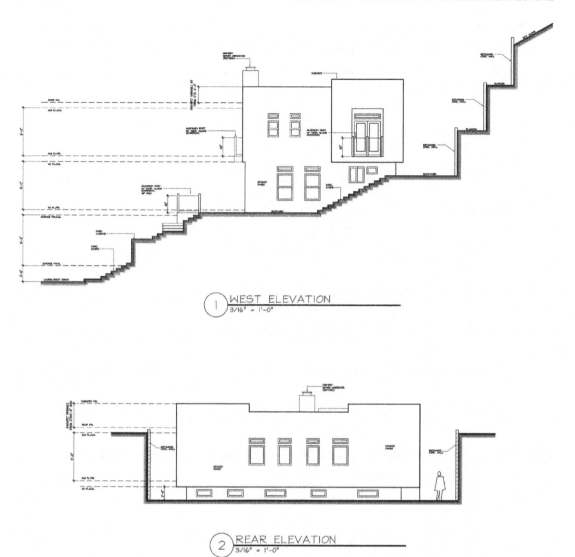

Figure 1-8. *West and rear elevation of the building (Courtesy of Afshin Kianpour)*

As you might have noticed, the side views of the building also show what seemed to be a flat surface in Figure 1-1, the topological land survey. Now we have a much better understanding of the building with its surroundings.

The last but not least important drawing in the barrage of architectural drawing is the cross-sectional view of the building. Figures 1-9 and 1-10 show the sections of the building that were marked in Figure 1-6 by the letters A and B.

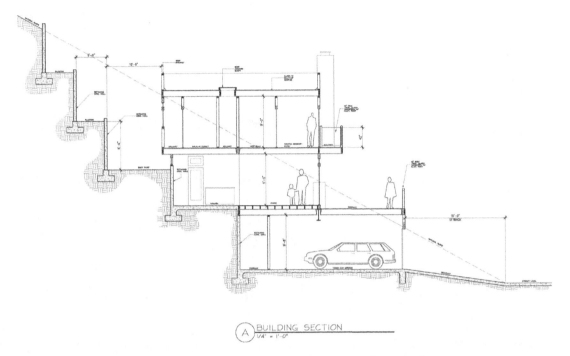

Figure 1-9. *Cross-section A of the building that was referenced in Figure 1-6 (Courtesy of Afshin Kianpour)*

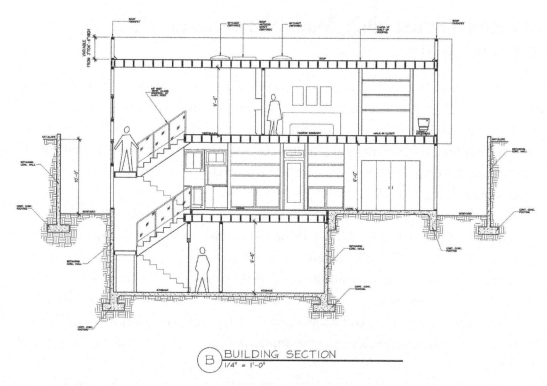

Figure 1-10. *Cross-sectional view of the building marked as B in Figure 1-6 (Courtesy of Afshin Kianpour)*

The cross-sectional drawings are vital among all architectural drawings because they provide insights where other drawings are not able to. The concept and application of a cross-sectional view of the system will come up in the later chapters. You will see how a vertical slice of the system creates not only an indication of how the system performs, but also it will create a cadence among the development team.

After the architectural drawings are made, reviewed, revised, and approved, they will be sent to the construction engineers for review and then are absolutely enforced on the construction site. No deviation from the prints without architects' approval is permitted. In addition, in case of confusion and doubt, construction engineers are responsible to consult with the architects to clarify and resolve the issues. The change orders must follow a formal approval process and all the changes in the plan are carefully documented. There are two types of drawings, the plans and the as-built. The plan is what is being ordered to the construction engineers to build and as-built is documenting what actually was built. The gap between plan and as-built is filled with the approved change orders.

Drawing's Reusability, Maintainability, Readability, and Scalability

Each booklet of architectural drawing is comprised of several layers that organize the drawings based on job functions involving their corresponding processes such as electrical, mechanical, HVAC, Fire and Safety, Security, Data, and so forth. For example, a typical architectural drawing might contain one or more of these layers: Architecture, Building Survey, Civil, Electrical, Landscape, Structural, Plumbing, Mechanical, Telecommunication, Data, etc.

The idea of creating layers is rather about having everything on one drawing; if you make each layer transparent, by stacking all the layers on top each other you can get a three-dimensional visualization of the building or what we call it today, a static simulation of the object. So basically it is civil engineering that pioneered the model simulation. Obviously engineers utilize this tool in order to find the design defects, establish guidelines, avoid reworks, and unify the language of people involved. This would leave no room for doubts and miscommunication. This would be the keystone of efficiency.

Each sheet of drawing is filled with symbols and lines. There is no unintended or meaningless line on the drawing pages. The symbols are consistent and unique throughout their representations and guided via legends. Above all, the flow of the diagrams is natural and intuitive and is intended to be understood by the engineers, technicians, and skilled workers who have limited or no related education.

Each page of drawing is marked with special guiding symbols to track down upstream and downstream drawings related to the page being studied. This unifies segregated drawings to one giant uniform road map to construct the building. In addition, the drawings help the building owners to maintain the building in years to come. For example, if years later there is a need for a major remodeling or reconstruction, then each drawing tells the story of what and where everything are. As you can see, many of the tools and methods that computer and software engineers use today are invented and initiated in the construction industry.

The numbering system and the modular approach to developing design documents somehow make the scaling of the design more convenient for the designers. There are sometimes even design considerations foreseen in the drawings for the expansion of the building. All the hooks and handles in each layer are to allow scalability either by merging with other modules or facilitating the merger of the future modules. The following image shows four layers of drawing for the same layout that they can get stacked up one on top of another. As we mentioned before, each layer is assigned only to one job function. For example, one layer can be architectural, the others, plumbing, electrical, and mechanical.

Figure 1-11 shows the stack of various building drawings. Starting from the architectural layer, the designed measure, and mark of the building perimeters, it utilizes the land surveying map from Figure 1-1. Then they slowly move into the building, designing the major spaces from living room and kitchen to closets and pantry. Once the spaces are marked then they look at functionality of each room in order to establish all the inputs and outputs to that room for which to satisfy the functionality requirements. Once all the inputs and outputs to the building are estimated, then functional drawings are introduced. For example, the data line might have its own drawing layer to feed data to various functional spaces across the house. Some of the layers are very recent due to the advancement in home automation and modern security functionalities that require their own set of special skills to meet some very complex requirements.

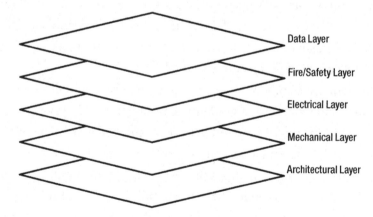

Figure 1-11. *The stack of various building drawing layers including architectural, mechanical, electrical, and so forth*

As you have observed so far, the building construction industry is much more advanced than what it looks like from the facade. This is because the facade of the building has stayed the same for thousands of years, but the building applications have greatly specialized. The secret for keeping up with modern-life demand while keep the same simple surface is that civil engineers are very familiar with modularity and work organization. The very pivotal point in building construction is in architecture, understanding the need of the application and clearly marking the boundaries of functionalities while keeping in mind that the entire work should be carried out in an undistributed work fashion utilizing various skill sets.

Making Buildings versus Making PCBs

The reason that the building industry has such a stiff approach toward doing the documentation before starting the construction is that the design deviation in a building construction can potentially cost the project its entire lifeline, or even worse, in some cases can bankrupt the company. When constructing a PCB, making a mistake, for example, in the layout of the PCB can only cost the company on average a few weeks delay and a few hundred dollars' worth of rework, which is nowhere close to cost of rework in a building construction. Yes, there have been catastrophic failures that cost nations billions of dollars and caused permanent environmental damage as a result of a single PCB failure, but we are talking about the cost of a project, not the liability cost of a product. In other words, the nature of developing real-time systems might give a false impression that we can successfully finish a failing product that passes all the phases of development but it can still fail miserably in the field.

Since the consequences of rework in a building are grave initially, civil engineers have many defined and strict design guidelines. But in embedded system development, the cost of rework and prototypes are much more manageable, which has led us to be more forgiving toward design mistakes and reworks. However, the real-time systems might not appear to carry a high up-front project cost, but the liability cost of embedded systems might be far greater exceeded than the liability costs of a building. This is why for the critical applications, we need more than an Agile developmental process to guarantee reliability of our product.

Summary

The topics discussed in this chapter were not covered in order to state the obvious about different industries, but to show some simple trends and to highlight some common challenges. What we think is a complicated problem in our industry might be just a norm in another industry. Electrical, computer, and software engineering are the professions of the 20th century and still in their infancy in terms of the level of maturity in establishing solid standards and methods compared to some other ancient professions. Some might even think that with the ever-changing face of our industry, there is a lot left to learn and we might never get to establish a one-method-fits-all stage.

CHAPTER 2

Project Management Methods

There are many ways to define and call a real-time system with respect to their intended applications, but in a general sense, as its name implies, it is a system that carries out applications that are dedicated, focused, and above all are time sensitive. Depending on how the application needs to be carried out, there are systems that must execute their tasks at certain times; some give you a range of time to execute an application, and the rest want you to execute the application but are not too pushy about it. They are called hard real-time systems, soft real-time systems, and general purpose computers respectively. Depending on who we consult with, there are a lot of discussions in categorizing the computer systems of which some get into deep philosophical discussions about the concept of time. For the sake of our discussion, the above definitions about real-time systems can suffice.

In old days, a real-time system was purely hardware based. A PID controller that had sets of screws, resistors, capacitors, and amplifiers with an almost infinitely fast control loop response was considered an embedded system. However, with all the perks that would come with the pure hardware-based controllers and by the invention of transistors, the designers decided to have software involved in order to make the systems user friendly and easier to maintain. Nowadays it is hard to imagine that a real-time system can operate without any embedded software.

The main objective to justify using a real-time system for an application is that these systems are application specific, which means you cannot utilize your personal computer to carry out its tasks. In addition, this translates to a system that benefits from a tightly designed hardware and software architecture. For example, an automobile's cruise control system is comprised of various hardware and software components that receive commands from the driver, data from various sensors, and performs a control algorithm for this specific application in order to monitor and maintain the speed of the vehicle.

© Mohsen Mirtalebi 2017
M. Mirtalebi, *Embedded Systems Architecture for Agile Development*,
https://doi.org/10.1007/978-1-4842-3051-0_2

The ease of use of digital systems; compact packaging; low cost of semiconductor devices such as microprocessors, microcontrollers, memory chips, solid state switches, and so forth has made the use of these transistor-based components in real-time industrial systems very popular. But all these benefits come with a cost, which is the cost of software development. Although this new branch of science – software engineering – is still at its initial stage compared to the other branches of science, the progress it has made and the lives it has touched already are far beyond other sciences.

As the science of software leaps toward more advancement, it branches into more specialty fields and takes on new names. In the meantime, more project/product management tools and methods are introduced to cope with this fast transient of progress. The following is only an introduction to some basic and related topics on the subject of embedded systems development.

The Basics

Whether we are all experts or rookies or anything in between in project management, we should agree on some common definitions. Let's all agree that a firmware is a special case of software that exclusively performs real-time applications and directly controls the machine on a time-critical and predictable basis. Although there are various definitions for what is called real time and what level of time criticality there is to it (hard or soft real time) but either way a real-time system is a system developed where the use of a PC or any other general purpose computers fail to deliver results in a predictable and deterministic manner.

Project Management Using Critical Path Methods (CPM)

To start off with the first and one of the oldest project management methods, we introduce critical path methods. This method has been used in many industries from construction to product development and any process that is based on a phase-gate approach.

What Is CPM?

CPM was initially invented around the 1940s and put in practice by the U.S. Navy for developing the Polaris Defense System. The magnitude of the project and its sensitivity, complexity, and criticality due to geopolitics of the time, which coincided with the height of the Cold War, is evident to the effectiveness of this powerful management tool. Unfortunately as it is the case for most functional methods and as the time passed, this tool became either overly complicated or simplified as it was slowly making headway into different industries.

The effectiveness of this tool became so popular among industries that even the construction industry started heavily utilizing the tools for resource scheduling. Although the CPM tool they used was a watered-down version of this version of time-series analysis, it still was proven to be very effective. This oversimplified the use of the tool and made this active tool to have a reactive personality in the face of changes in the project. The people who took the tool seriously and wanted a more proactive role for it became so obsessed with the tool that they forgot analysis, creating graphs and reports are not the objectives of the tool.

The rest in the industry use the tool as an intimidation tool to induce productivity in human resources. The overcomplication in the tool made the method heavy in documentations, which in turn made it costly to maintain and slow to respond to changes. The oversimplified methods carry little to no effectiveness due to the lack of a realistic outlook toward inevitable and constant changes which proven to be excessively stiff toward adapting the changes. Maybe this is the reason the construction industry found it effective as the culture in that industry is inflexible toward changes.

Creating a Robust Gantt Chart

The Gantt chart is the most widely used and, in some cases, abused project management tool in the history of management. If someone asks us to name a management tool common between a project with a goal of developing a hi-tech medical product and developing a new hospital building, the answer would be a Gantt chart. Although a Gantt chart is only one of the graphical representations of a project in CPM, it is by far the most popular and effective tool for planning, tracking, and forecasting a project.

The Gantt chart is enormously effective if it is deployed and implemented correctly. A well-established Gantt chart can help the managers with their projects' bottlenecks and provide them with fairly accurate cost and time estimation and predictions. The principals of developing an effective Gantt chart are simple and intuitive. These can apply to any type of project: from developing a highly complex real-time system to a project comprised of writing a book.

Work Breakdown Structures (WBS)

If you refer to our initial discussion in the introduction chapter of the book, you see we distinguished between project and product developments. However from the CPD standpoint, these two terms are viewed the same and used interchangeably. Therefore the WBS contains both product and process breakdown structures. Contrary to popular belief, a manager shouldn't know everything about the work but should know who knows what. Task delegation is one of the manager's responsibilities but not for project planning. A project manager interviews the subject matter experts, observes work and time, and decides how to plan the project. Creating a WBS is one of the initial and essential activities a manager does to build a framework for the project at the planning phase.

Although the scope of the project is still to develop a product, later the process takes the upper hand and overshadows the product. Therefore a manager starts with identifying product functions and then plan resources based on those specific functions. For this, the first step would logically become interviewing the subject matter experts to identify the scope of the project and to gather enough data to create high-level product specifications, then slowly to break down the major parts to smaller pieces. For developing each part of the product, the project manager assigns some activities and tasks. It is how the resource planning is introduced to the project. When the resources, money, and time are assigned to the activities, then the process management takes the higher priority over the product management and that's how we get to where we are today, using Gantt charts for everything.

In project management the activity of decomposing processes to activities and then tasks is called creating a work breakdown structure. The WBS starts from the top processes and then continues down to creating subordinate task units that normally are assigned to or performed by a single individual for a certain duration of time. In industrial engineering the act of creating tasks for individuals in a top-down, functional, and homogeneous manner is part of work standardization. Normally work standardization is for a production environment where the flow of product is steady and work fluctuations are minimized. But if we assume a project is a one-time production, then most of work and time study techniques can apply.

The WBS development in analogy is similar to brainstorming or writing a journal or a book, starting from the title then moving on to subject of each chapter and eventually to the subjects of each paragraph. At this phase of planning, the project manager/author should not worry about the orders of the tasks and their relationships, rather utilizing their entire brain power to identify the works and to narrow down the project scope. But it is very unlikely that a writer is able to identify the topic of each paragraph at this early stages of a book's planning. However, whether it's true or not, the project managers get into their project planning stage, hoping they can identify all the functions and features of the product down to its nuts and bolts by systematically decomposing the functions to modules and components and the processes to activities and tasks in which all tasks carry an equal weight, are homogeneous, and take the same amount of time and resources. We all know that this hope never materializes but this is the underlying theory of project planning.

The decomposition method that we have discussed is centered on the product function. There are many ways other than function-based decomposition of a project. Some organizations might plan their product development based on their available resources, some based on their organizational charts, and some based on geographical regions or a combination of all these. Our WBS development is based on product function and we did this because we wanted to avoid waste by using just enough resources to carry out the tasks in full. Now let's assume that for writing this book, we need to create a WBS. Since we don't know how exactly the project would lay out, we base our best guesses on the major product functions.

There is a new idea and we want to introduce our new idea to our ever idea-hungry market. Therefore everything should revolve around expressing this new idea; otherwise we didn't have any reason to write a book about. However, we can't just expose our naked idea to the public. We are to dress it up decently and in layers so the reader would get engaged with the book as s/he goes through these familiar layers until it gets to the core idea. Therefore, introducing the new idea would be the main engine that drives writing this book, and as a rule of writing we should stay focused to the main scope of this book throughout writing all the chapters, even when we try to review the old and existing ideas that might be familiar and redundant to the majority of the readers. This is to keep the readers focused on the main topic of the book.

While performing WBS we should always have the project's scopes in mind; otherwise it is easy to get distracted, which will result in creating unnecessary functions and tasks. A well-defined project is not a project heavy on documentation: it is a project that is focused on only project scopes and deliverables. Since there are activities that are not directly related to project scopes and deliverables, but since they support activities and materials in order to deliver the project, therefore they should be built into the WBS. For example, for a construction project the delivery of all raw materials to the building site is a supporting activity. This needs to be included into the WBS so it is considered for the planning and scheduling phase. So the project's scope not only includes the WBS of the direct project tasks but also every aspect of the project whether they support the project directly or indirectly.

In Figure 2-1, the WBS of the direct contents for writing this book is used as an example without mentioning the indirect activities such as editing, which are vital to the delivery of quality contents. Also the main function of the book is to introduce a new idea; however the introduction and basics sections are the supporting functionalities in order to prepare the reader for the complex topics discussed in the "A New Idea" and "How It Works" sections. An additional advantage for utilizing WBS is to create a smooth flow in developing the more complex functions as well as tracing back all the points discussed in the advanced chapters back to the principals, making a solid point as you will. It also helps the designers to understand the requirements thoroughly without entangling into unnecessary details while missing on the major deliverables. The fruit of the matter is this: if you have a clear WBS you can easily explain your product, idea, function, in one sentence. It may be long but it will be all inclusive.

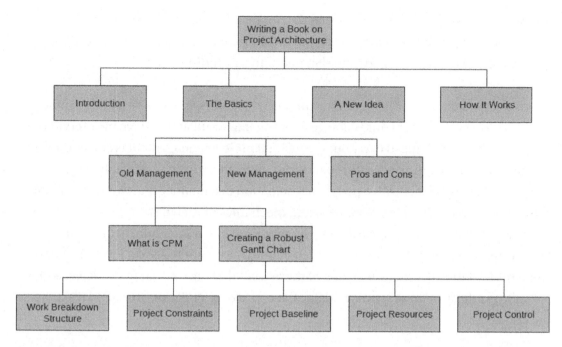

Figure 2-1. *Work breakdown of writing a book (Please note the entire project is not included)*

There are not enough words as to how important a WBS is to a product's development. It will clarify the path of development, identify the loopholes and resource constraints, and give a rough estimate of overall project time and resources needed or even a budget estimate if you have done similar projects. All in all, a WBS is the cornerstone of a successful product development process.

Project Constraints

After the majority of a project's tasks are identified, the project manager is responsible for applying project constraints to the tasks. Constraints are delicate affairs in every project. They define correlations among the tasks and are categorized to two types: physical and logical constraints. As an example for both cases, let's consider a project comprising tasks for staining a newly cemented floor. The physical constraint tells us that the floor can't be stained before the cement is actually made. In other words, it is impossible to stain the floor until the cement is poured and the actual floor comes into existence. You might laugh at this but you'll be surprised how many project managers forget this obvious fact. This is like adding more resources to a late project to make it go faster. As a rule of thumb, adding resources to a late project make it even later.

An example of a logical constraint is that the floor can't be stained until the cement is well cured. It is possible to stain a wet concrete floor but it normally doesn't lead to a good quality of paint plus a concrete slap needs to stay moist with water to cure for a while.

Although defining and categorizing project constraints are not as easy as it sounds here, a visionary manager could achieve a reasonable result at this stage by interviewing the people who are going to carry out the tasks. If project management is considered a combination of art and science, this part is definitely the artistic side of it. Because this is the part that asks for effective people participation in a manner that would reveal the actual costs, time, dynamics, resources, and mechanics of each task.

The WBS that we defined earlier can be projected into a schedule that is bounded by realistic constraints. The titles in bold in Figure 2-2 are not tasks as they carry some elements underneath. There are some of these tasks that have no room to wiggle, and as a result, any delay in these tasks can delay the entire project. These are called tasks on the critical path.

	Week1	Week2	Week3	Week4	Week5	Week6	Week7	Week8
Writing a Book On Management								
Introduction	▰							
The Basics								
Vintage Management								
What is CPM	▰							
Creating a Robust Gantt Chart								
Work Breakdown Structure		▰						
Project Constraints			▰					
Project Baseline				▰				
Project Resources					▰			
Project Control						▰		
New Management	▰	▰	▰	▰				
Pros and Cons							▰	▰
A New Idea	▰	▰	▰	▰				
How It Works						▰	▰	

Figure 2-2. *Gantt chart representation of an earlier WBS with an emphasis on time*

A Gantt chart can have more than one critical path and there are many methods to resolve a situation like this, which is beyond the scope of this book. However, as you can see in Figure 2-2, a simplified version of a project has been represented. This graph does not carry information on resources since there is only a person who was responsible to carry out this project. It also does not carry budgetary data and equipment utilization information. The more a Gantt chart is loaded with the information, the more realistic your project plan would become.

Project Resource Planning

Loading resources into the project schedule equips the Gantt chart with reality. There is no project with unlimited resources. Of all the available resources to any project, human resources are most valuable. The diligence, intelligence, and hard work of these resources have added some bright pages to the history of mankind. However, with all the advantages come some disadvantages as well. Human resources are unpredictable because they come with different strengths and weaknesses and are prone to sudden tiredness, mistakes, and illnesses. Therefore, project managers often assign a separate calendar to these resources that are different from the project calendar. It's called a resource calendar.

After loading the resources to the Gantt chart, the nature of the project schedule changes and it becomes a controllable entity. Now the project managers can forecast the final budget and time; increase or decrease the scopes of the project; outsource or in-source activities; and effectively manage the resources, controlling time and budget.

Project Control

Project control in its classical definition deals with three major constraints – time, cost, and quality – where changing one will affect the other two. But let's have in mind that the purpose of project control is to find the optimum point where all these three intersect, creating a project minimized in budget and time and maximized in quality. After the resources are loaded into the project, a manager can control any of these constraints. For example, for a better quality product, a project manager can place quality control processes in the schedule that will prolong the project and impose more costs or have it to speed up so s/he can remove some product features or minimize the scope.

Another art of project management is to minimize the cost of the project where it's possible. Leveling the resources ensures the maximized utilization of the resources by adjusting the occurrence of the tasks by sliding them back and forth within their time buffer without affecting downstream tasks. This is called resource leveling. Performing the project leveling task is tedious and delicate. As you move the task within its allowable time window, you have to go back and adjust every other task in the project accordingly. This is where the computer programs can help with automatically adjusting the project. There are different techniques as for resource leveling; you can divide or combine tasks, reduce or increase scopes, or add or remove resources to it such as outsourcing or in-sourcing the tasks. Figure 2-3 shows the famous project management triangle that each project is believed to be affected by. It is not possible that any side of the triangle can be modified without affecting the other two sides.

Figure 2-3. *The project management pyramid*

At the end, CPM is a tool that would give us enough control to make educated decisions to manipulate the project in a safe and controlled fashion. It was created to just do that in order to minimize the risk of the decision-making process and to lead a project to the optimum point where the cost and time are minimized and the quality is maximized.

Project Management Using Agile Methods

Although Agile methods were primarily invented to manage software development processes rather than firmware, more and more hi-tech companies have adopted them for developing their real-time applications. In the early 2000s several software engineers published a manifesto for Agile methodologies that summarize the unified philosophies supporting these methods. The manifesto especially emphasizes individualism, light documentations, more interaction with the customers, and adapting changes on the go rather than following a set plan such as a V-Model. There are books written on this subject and reiterating those topics is beyond the scope of book. We just touch up a few related topics on this subject and then move on to other parts.

What Does Agile Mean?

Agile, as it is evident from its name, means fast response to the customers' needs. However the term is effectively used in the software development, while in manufacturing it is interchangeably used with the lean term. In general any system that has specialized tools and methods to respond quickly to changes is called Agile. This is like the hundred-meter Olympics runners who possess the right muscle tone, weight, and height and are physically different from the marathon runners who are lean and slow; therefore agility implies efficiency, having just the right gears for the challenge ahead. There are many different methods under the Agile umbrella such as Kanban, Scrum, FDD, DSDM, ASD, XP, Lean, Crystal, and more. If we understand the reasoning behind Agile methodologies, we can apply one methodology or a combination of methodologies to make our process efficient in function and responsive to unexpected issues. For the sake of our argument we picked Scrum to discuss.

The Ideal Scrum

Scrum is one of more the popular Agile approaches to software development. Although Scrum is very receptive to changes, it has its own shortcomings in adapting to real-world problems. The ideal Scrum is for a team of five to nine people with T-shape skill sets who perform a daily stand-up meeting and periodical sprints every two to three weeks. The main theme in Scrum is repetition, gathering momentum of generating results, and adding values to the product in small increments. At the end of each cycle the team produces something that they like to call a Potentially Shippable Product. The team is required to perform the cycles of inspect and adapt when they are taking on their tasks. The ideal Scrum works as a management tool such as CPM and as a product development framework such as CPD; however the methods to function as a framework, especially when it comes to budgeting and planning, have not been fully clear.

Scrum Master

Although Scrum seems to be trying to avoid creating a project management position in its classical form, in which the project manager would top the hierarchy of the project organization, in the real world it faces some challenges due to the fact that the massive antiquated financial systems and majority of project stakeholders still like to respond to the older project structures. As a result the Scrum Master is the one who usually has to put multiple hats on. The primary role of a Scrum master is to act as a facilitator to the team to remove impediments, shield the team from outside influences, keeps the team focused during daily stand-ups, and acts as a public relations person on behalf of the team at the stakeholders' meetings.

Project Backlog

Backlog is the process of creating a work breakdown structure in a way that the created tasks can be ideally completed during one sprint by a single developer. Sprint is the unit of time in Scrum and normally has a fixed time span of two to three weeks. The team's performance and velocity and projected completion time is expressed in Sprints. Sometimes during the sprint the team members get together to refine the stories, their orders and definitions, objectives, and score them as the project unfolds and more details become available to the team. This creates a need for another Scrum process that is called Backlog Grooming.

Sprint Planning

After the backlog is created and organized in an open and relaxed fashion, it is presented to the team member at each sprint planning session. The term "relaxed" is to oppose any excessive planning ahead of time by meticulously arranging the backlog items in any particular order. This stage of the process is comparable to the stage in the Gantt chart process where the PM interviews the team members to identify the constraints and time required to complete each task. Since the emphasis is on individualism, the team memebers decide what to do first and it happens right at the planning stage. Also note each task in Scrum is called a Story and carries two values, weight and an estimated time to complete the tasks. The weight of the project is used to create an estimated completion time for important milestones in the project.

Project Control

Although it might not be evident from the Scrum's streamline that the process is being controlled, it is. It's being done through different interfaces, tools, and methods.

- The Done-Done List

  This is practically a quality node in the process. The done list is a list of objectives and qualifications that is used to qualify whether a sprint task is complete. Creating these subtasks is not mandatory and it is at a developer's discretion to use them in order to satisfy the objectives that have been set by the stakeholders/product owner to qualify the task as complete. It is also called an acceptance criterion for any story. Mentioning the word "Done" twice is to emphasize the importance of completeness of the task at the end of the sprint, which lends its existence to the concept of "potentially shippable product."

- Potentially Shippable Product

  This part works as resource leveling during developing the Gantt chart. The developmental tasks performed during each sprint are to produce enough incremental progress in software features that the product can be shipped to the customers at the end of the sprint. The product might not carry all the features that the stakeholders have in mind, but it is a complete working small-scale (in features) product. We will discuss this concept in a greater detail in the next chapters.

- Team Members Co-locations

  Scrum process requires the team members to be located close to each other in order to perform effective daily stand-up meetings.

- Daily Stand-Ups

  During the Sprint, each team member is required to participate in the daily meetings, preferably early on the work schedule. Then each member will briefly explain three things: what has been done from the last stand-up, what is going to be done after this stand-up, and whether there are any impediments that prevent this team member from achieving his/her goals. Daily stand-ups are meant to inform the stakeholders about the pace of the project and potential problems.

- Sprint Review/Retrospective

    This is a meeting scheduled after the Sprint is done. The team decides if each story is completed based on the done-done list. Also the team members are provided a chance to give input to the stakeholders on how the overall process can be improved.

- Cost, Quality, Time, and Scope

    In traditional project management the scope of the project is normally a set value, and at least less evident as a tool for the project manager to steer the project. In Scrum, the scope of the project is a more pronounced value and more readily available to the managers than the earlier management methods. The Scope of the project is normally divided to two, Must-Have, and Nice-To-Have attributes for each Story and there will be two projections toward the end of the project for each category (see Figure 2-4). The smaller triangle is representative of Must-Have scope and the larger triangle represents the Nice-To-Have scope, which engulfs the smaller scope. It is worthy of mention that the scopes never change during the run of a Sprint.

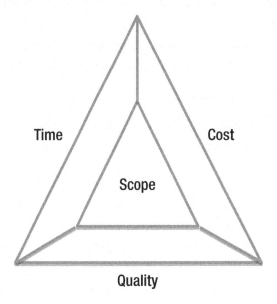

Figure 2-4. *An Agile process control pyramid*

- Burn-Down/Up Charts

  The team members are required to log their activities and progress by entering hours spent and left to finish each task of the story. As a result the Scrum master is able to graph the projected completion of each story in order to track down the progress toward each Sprint, Release, or Project end dates. In addition, by accumulating all the tasks done, the stakeholders are able to measure the average speed of the team and project the dates.

- Cone of Uncertainty

  Software development in Agile utilizes a graph known as "The Cone of Uncertainty" to describe how a project is being dynamically sized in terms of time, cost, and scope (see Figure 2-5). As the project progresses from concept to test, the amount of certainty reduces in scope, cost, and time of the project.

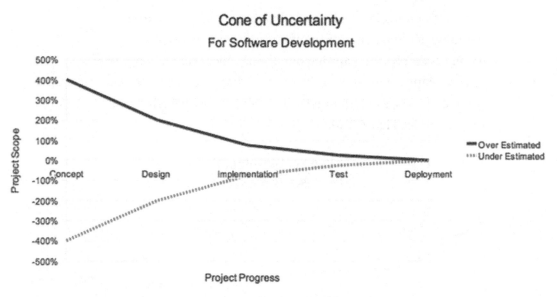

Figure 2-5. *Cone of uncertainty for any product development: in this case, software*

However, if there are extra efforts spent at the design stage the benefit would be a much narrower uncertainty at the earlier stage of the project. This does not mean that an earlier stage of the project phase equates to an earlier milestone on the project time line since this often causes the design stage to become longer in time; on the other hand, the implementation, test, and deployment phases will shrink in time.

Although Agile methodologies claim that they are light on documentations unlike other traditional methods, this graph is evidence that they unofficially support requirement analysis. Again, this is from the software engineering perspective regarding software projects. Nevertheless due to the nature of real-time systems, the use of clear requirement specifications is vital for communications and scope definitions.

- Release Planning

Release planning is a high-level plan that is a subset of project planning. It often contains many sprints and it has all the elements for project planning but on a smaller scale. Therefore a release planning must include a set of prioritized and estimated product backlogs and defined scopes, schedules, velocity, and resources (see Figure 2-6).

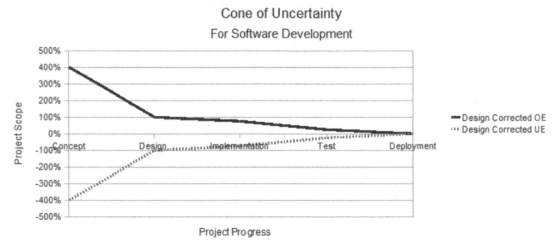

Figure 2-6. *Cone of uncertainty when more time is spent on design phase*

Collaborative Product Development (CPD)

Every year in the United States there are thousands of patent applications being filed. From all these applications only a selected few become manufacturable and also profitable. Therefore one might view CPD as a financial tool for funding and representing various complex apparatuses of a project in an abstract form. Therefore CPD is more of financial tool than a developmental one to size up the worth of new concepts for investment purposes. However one of its useful by products is that it gives an architectural view of the product. If we assume CPM and Scrum are the vehicles carrying the project/product from concept to release, CPD is the road map.

Firmware is one of the most important building blocks of a real-time system; that's why it must be viewed from a broader perspective and in the context of other major elements such as manufacturing, purchasing, hardware development, and so forth. CPD brings all these aspects of product development efforts together under one umbrella in a presentable and understandable fashion to the project stakeholders.

Aside from the financial aspect of a CPD, which looks a lot like a business plan, there are many aspects of which they are technical and related to product development. There are normally five to six phases and gates associated with the entire process (see Figure 2-7). Phases comprised of activities and deliverables and gates are for the executive managers to decide whether to allow the project to move on, postponed, reduced in scope, or canceled.

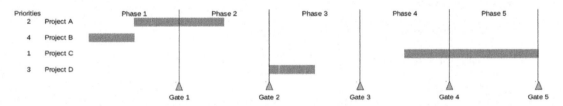

Figure 2-7. *Typical phases of a CPD process*

This representation of the project is specifically crafted for the executive managers since they oversee many concurrent projects at a given time. It enables them to visually track down the progress made. It actually is a super project of all projects in a pseudo-Gantt chart format. These bars depict a snapshot of progress to date with respect to the phases and gates.

Tasks, Deliverables, and Decisions

There are many different opinions and philosophical points of view on CPD process. The following is a very simplified version of it that emphasizes only major and conventionally agreeable highlights in the process. CPD is focused heavily on documentations, the same as any business plan submitted to an angle investor or a bank for the purpose of seeking seed money for a start-up business.

The bankers and investors might not have a clue about what the loan applicant is planning to really do with the money but the order and amount of documentations tells them if the applicant has done his/her homework and if s/he is ready to unleash all her/his resources to have a successful project. This is a natural process to minimize the risk and protect the investment. The following is a summary of a general CPD process.

Phase One (Concept Development)

- Tasks:

   Defining Customer Requirements

   Developing Proof of Concept

   Intellectual Property Study

   Developing Product Quality Metrics

- Deliverables:

   Marketing Requirement Specifications

   Concept Prototypes

   IP Report

   Marketing Test Specifications

Gate One

Making decisions based on all the deliverables regarding market feasibility, product manufacturability, IP clearances, technology availability, and a clear regulatory path.

Phase Two (Project/Product Planning and Architecture)

- Tasks:

   Project Planning Including Development, Manufacturing, Regulatory, and Quality/Reliability Planning

   Developing Product Architectural Plan included with the functional modules and components and also Risk Management Study

- Deliverables:

   All Project, Manufacturing, and Regulatory Plans and Risk Assessments

   All Architectural Documents including Modules and Component Requirements and Test Specs

Gate Two

The simple decision at this stage is to answer whether the product is manufacturable? To come to an educated decision is to develop and review all the documents generated at this stage. This is a lengthy process but is the path of least resistance; should the product fail further down the line it will cost the company a lot more.

Phase Three (Design)

- Tasks:

   Design Modules and Models

   DFMEA

   Design Reviews

   Software Development

   Developing Pilot Manufacturing Lines

   Developing V&V Specs

- Deliverables:

    Generating Documents for all the above tasks

    Developing Hardware Prototypes

    Developing Design Documents, Codes, Models, and Modules

Gate Three

Design Freeze and Moving Forward into Manufacturing

Phase Four (V&V and Optimization)

- Tasks:

    Performing Software and Hardware V&V

    Developing PFMEA

    Software Optimization

    Engineering and Reliability Testing

    Regulatory Submissions

    Manufacturing Pilot Run and Test Design

- Deliverables:

    Test Results and Design Modification recommendations

Gate Four

This involves making decisions if the tests are performed sufficiently, design changes are valid, and regulatory testing are qualified. Is the Vendor Selected? Is the Manufacturing Process Stable?

Phase Five (Product Launch)

- Tasks:

    Developing Customer Manuals and Training them

    Developing Service Plans

    Filed Tests

- Deliverables:

  Generating Field Test Report

  Documenting the Manufacturing Process

Gate Five

Is the Project Close-Out, Audit, and Design Transfer Complete?

As we saw in the past CPD summary, we can see how a project is comprised of various engineering disciplines and how people outside of the circle of the project view its wholeness as a coherent entity. In addition, the tedious documentation process is viewed as a form of communication where it unifies perceptions, declares definitions, and answers questions. But to an engineer, the documentation process should be more than that. It should also be about benchmarking, calculating, and arriving to the same conclusion as planned. No matter how much effort an engineer puts in defining the objectives, it is always easier than troubleshooting and less expensive than reworks.

Software and Project Management

Since the science of software is very new compared to mathematics and physics, and also it is rapidly evolving, the impact of software on the projects has been underestimated by the popular belief. However the impact is being noticed by more companies. The main problem with real-time system development projects is that software seems to be always on the critical path and often creating a long bottleneck for the product on the way to market. In addition the quality software has been of a concern more so than other major components such as hardware. This is because there is a great hole in the software project management and even more in how to integrate the software development in a project where what we all are used to seeing are tangible and quick results. For this let's have a very general look into the software structure of a real-time system.

Software Layers

In a real-time system, depending on its application, there might be up to three major and distinct levels of software: algorithm firmware, system firmware, and application software. Without getting into the details, for example, in a cruise control system the algorithm firmware would contain the control algorithm. The system firmware then would be in charge of peripheral management and communications to the sensors and vehicle's main processor. Finally the application software is one that runs on the main computer to collect, report, and perform general housekeeping activities for the network of various real-time subsystems. However application software is also referred to as the software that connects a real-time system to a general purpose processor such as a personal computer that runs with a non-real-time operating system. These pieces of real-time system firmware that are connected to the PC are often called drivers.

In Figure 2-8 the sensors transfer their data to the system firmware portion of an embedded system and consequently the core firmware of it in order to carry a specific function. The combination of the hardware and software for this embedded system normally runs on a real-time basis. Sometimes in larger machines several of these embedded systems need to communicate with a larger processor for coordination, monitoring, and reporting purposes. The host computer often needs not to be a real-time system. The smaller embedded systems are called the driver for the general purpose computer that would run specific applications in a timely manner then report the results to the main computer. The main computer is the one that normally would interface with the user to report the total system conditions.

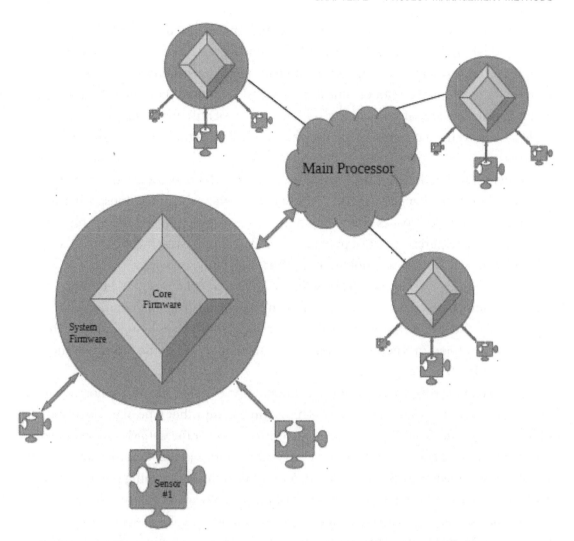

Figure 2-8. *Hardware-dependent software layout for an embedded system*

Software Development Process

As we mentioned earlier, software engineering is a very new discipline in the engineering world but has gained a tremendous amount of attention and applications. This rapid explosion in growth has caused the software engineering to get ahead of its standardization process and best practices simply because by the time the rules of the games are invented, the playground has changed.

Compare this with very stable and relatively unchanged engineering disciplines such as civil or mechanical. In these fields the standards and procedures are well defined and tools and processes of engineering have been modernized, but the logic behind them has stayed relatively the same. For example, to build a house 20 years ago you needed a blueprint. Today you also need the same thing to start a house although the architectural plans and drawings might not be blue anymore and are replaced by fancy 3D animation along complex structural simulations; but the process of building is still the same. To build a house you need architectural drawings regardless of the color or format of the drawings.

As mentioned in the introduction of the book, a builder needs a 2D drawing of the floor plans with all measurements. The plan must show the utility lines, structural elements, and defined spaces along their purposes. It also should include the materials used. Then the requirements, test plans, and regulatory processes including city, state, and federal codes need to be implemented and noted in the drawings.

Building a single-family ranch house faces different regulations than building a movie theater. These codes and regulations can change the order of execution of the project tasks and also greatly impacts the materials and processes being utilized. This can delay the project and add unwanted costs if the initial plan of the project has not been studied well.

In civil engineering, lack of proper documentation equates directly to money, time, quality, and in most cases safety issues. This is true for any other type of engineering projects and so the same for software engineering. However the behavior that some of the major software companies have created is a false public perception that software shouldn't be perfect the first time around. As a result various governing bodies of this profession have tried to create road maps for a proper software development process.

One of these attempts was to create and recommend the software companies to adhere to software life-cycle processes. One of the more recent (still in software space it's considered ancient) procedures is V-Model for software development. The reason V-Model is being discussed here is that it is much more aligned with CPD and Agile processes than other product life cycles such as waterfall or spiral. Again there are many different types of V-Model implementations. However for the purpose of simplicity we have brought here a version that is most common.

Software Reusability, Maintainability, Readability, and Scalability

In the real-time systems the spirit of software flows throughout the entire product development life cycle from part qualification to prototyping, hardware design, algorithm simulations, system troubleshooting, engineering and manufacturing tests, field diagnostics, and so on. The idea is to make the software reusable in a way that as product passes through the phases of the development the software module would only require it to be added together or trimmed to fit that particular phase. For example, the software at the prototyping stage can be used for the product's algorithm and system firmware, then to be modified for engineering and manufacturing tests.

Software reusability and scalability in conjunction with developing a clear architectural road map will spread the software development efforts across the product life cycle rather than putting it in front of the project to create bottlenecks. In CPM, software development is often highlighted on a critical path that leads to more project delays that will result in a delayed product release to the market. Software reusability, scalability, and readability in the spirit of DFM will also introduce consistency to the project, preventing waste in time and materials, which consequently reduces or even eliminates reworks. In addition, it allows engineers to establish a benchmarking process for product's functions at the concept and design stage that would result in a more reliable product with less field returns and greater features for the customers, especially in product diagnostics.

There is often a misunderstanding for distinguishing between reusability and scalability. The goal in utilizing reusability in a software is not to use the entire software program wholly in all phases of the product life cycle but to create features that easily allow the designers to scale up or back to the extent that would not lose its main functional characteristics while serving a function. You don't need the engine of an 18-wheeler on a VW Beetle.

Software throughout CPD Process

As we've seen earlier the simplified CPD process would have five different and distinct phases for product development: concept, architecture, design, validation/verification/ optimization, and product launch. Modern real-time systems benefit from software in all these phases:

- Software for Product Concept

  Simulation and analysis and algorithm development software are extensively utilized for proof of concept for a new product.

- Software for Product Architecture

  Using Modeling Languages and high-level languages with custom-made graphical user interfaces, external database interfacing, connectivity to the outside world, and operating systems glue various modules.

- Software for Product Design

  Firmware and low-level programing languages are used to make the product function based on its defined requirements.

- Software for Validation/Verification/Optimization

  Various engineering and reliability testing including software regression, highly accelerated life testing (HALT), and smoke testing are being used to run extended automated test scripts that run for hours or sometimes days to test various functionalities of the system prototypes.

- Software for Product Launch

  In manufacturing testing, normally automated test equipment is utilized for final checks before shipping the product to the customer. When the product is in the field, the asset management and user-interface software are used to provide system monitoring and diagnostics utilities.

V-Model (Software Life Cycle)

Like any other classical methods a V-Model has a top-down approach for product development. The model was invented to manage developing a system, not just particularly a software system; however it's more popular now in the software development domain since it originated from there. Therefore the underlying principles of a V-Model can apply to any system development whether it is hardware, manufacturing, finance, or arts. Keep in mind there is no single, accepted definition of this model. Many government agencies such as the FDA require adopting a product life-cycle process as a prerequisite to obtain proper certifications for the product. There are also many international institutions that won't give your product their stamp of approval unless a well-documented product life cycle is demonstrated.

The V-Model is highly document oriented. The entire left branch of the model, which is more than half of development, is focused on design definitions, specifications, and requirements including creating documents for the right branch. Products that closely follow a well-established V-Model normally have a significant longer design phase and much shorter implementations and integrations phases, which normally receive a higher product quality mark in the field. This is because the process has an iterative nature between all the phases involved in the process.

The hierarchical nature of this model implies a work breakdown structure similar to the CPM method. The architectural stage is comprised of many modules and then modules are broken down to components and so forth in the requirement and design phases.

As you can see, the majority of the design branch is assigned to creating various design documents. This means that at the start of the project the developers do not get the chance to implement and test any code until later at the implementation level. Therefore the majority of design is conceptual and abstract. For example, when the developers define the modules' functions, they also create design documents for it along the test specifications. This will cause the developers to conceptualize the product in finer detail before developing the real product but at the end, the product definitions, like a well-designed rocket once it's fueled, will take off on an incredible speed into the implementation and integration.

Nevertheless there is a great chance that at the implementation level, the designers need to go back to the corresponding documents and update them for the design changes. This also applies to the opposite branch denoted as a test. The circular arrows are to highlight the feedback and feed forward nature of each phase of the V-Model with respect to the preceding and succeeding phases as well as parallel phases on the test branch (see Figure 2-9).

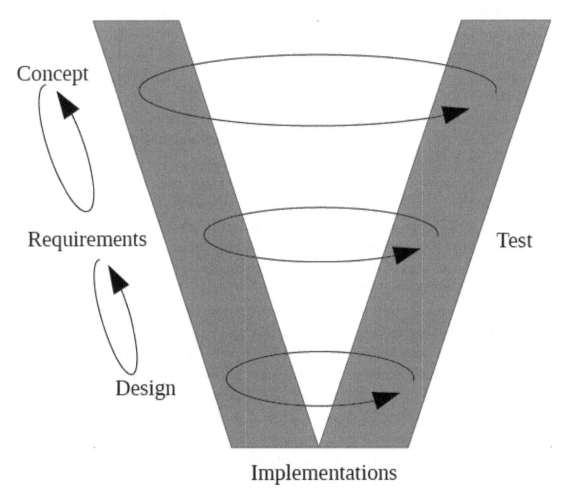

Figure 2-9. *A typical V-Model for a software development process*

Design for Manufacturing (DFM)

Design for manufacturing is a proactive concept that instills the idea of manufacturing in the earliest stages of product development. After all, the inventors create ideas so they can be manufactured and widely used. A very simplified version of DFM principals follows.[1] Please note these concepts not only apply to physical hardware but also to software in many ways. The developers must do the following:

- Reduce the total number of parts. The fewer parts, the fewer vendors to deal with, qualify, employ, communicate, and monitor. Also fewer parts mean fewer reasons for the product to malfunction or fail in the field.

- Develop a modular design. All parts shouldn't be ready at the same time but a placeholder can be designed so it keeps manufacturing ready for the final launch rather than dumbing everything on manufacturing all at once.

- Use of standard components. Consider the End of Life of components and parts, pricing, and logistics. Introducing new parts to the existing manufacturing system is expensive.

- Design parts to be multifunctional. For example, a heat sink might also function as a structural element to support parts.

- Design parts for multiuse. The multiuse parts can be used in different products.

- Design for ease of fabrication.

- Design with standard interfaces. For example, if one of the communication protocols is CAN, try to utilize this protocol for subassembly, firmware download, and user-interface communications for as much as possible. The less costume interfaces, the less integration and troubleshooting problems.

- Maximize compliance by following one standard process, tool, and method from design to manufacturing. This minimizes human errors.

There is much more to the DFM concept, but what is mentioned above applies to designing and manufacturing real-time systems.

Modeling Languages and Agile

Modeling languages are firmware programming tools that allow the firmware developers to graphically design, implement, simulate, and test the software independent of the target hardware. Although bringing up the concept of development tools might seem irrelevant to the topic of project architecture, the impact that these tools have on the project structure, development, time, budget, and quality necessitates a short mention of their huge benefits. Because of the scope of these tools and their numerous features and their inherently compatible nature with Agile software development methods, a good project architect can combine all the phases of the entire left side of the V-Model by combining concept, requirements, design, and implementations all in one phase.

Unified Modeling Language (UML)

The idea of unified modeling language has been around for a while; however the tool is a registered trademark of IBM. Now many companies have invented their own UML type of tools. The idea behind UML and other comparable tools are to allow the user to define a system in a graphical format and convert, simulate, and test the graphics or the program scripts. The program script is a result of automatic conversion from graphics to a textual program.

Model-Based Design (MBD)

Model-based design is a subset of the modeling languages. You can define a system in terms of its control diagrams by utilizing finite state machines, math functions, and formulas, or a combination of all and generate program codes from them. The advantage of utilizing MBD is that the researchers and/or designers can simulate the results and establish benchmarks for the design validation and verification phases for the entire development process until the end – meaning the same benchmarking can be used from concept until deployment and even in the field for diagnostics and preventative maintenance.

There are many advantages to using model-based design for real-time system development; however the detail of the tool utilization is not in the scope of this book. As we discussed before the MBD tools are well compatible with Agile product development processes while saving money and lives.

Summary

The Scrum functions the best for pure software projects where the co-location of the team members is possible. However they are not suitable for multidisciplinary, safety-critical projects such as firmware development where the software and hardware are developed at the same time in different development campuses. If a video game crashes, it can restart again with minimal bodily harm to the user; but in case of an electric motor's catastrophic failure, the extent of the damages can be unimaginable.

Although the spirit of Scrum aligned with the principles of DFM and asks for an all-hands collaboration among all the various functional teams and stakeholders, in reality the majority of Scrum meetings suffer from lack of stakeholder participation. Mainly the assumption in a Scrum setup is to gather program specialist with related fields of expertise in one place. This often leaves the manufacturing and purchasing departments out. As often, it's the case with the design engineers, who start their career right after they leave their desk at school, so they have minimal contact with real-world problems. Enforcing DFM concepts in a development team environment will make the design ideas grounded and practical.

Another aspect of CPD that suffers in a Scrum environment is optimization. In simple language, we all know when the marketing engineers see the product prototypes they want to ship to the customers. This inherent rush in Agile processes will make the optimization phase with less importance in the eyes of the sales team. This is because the optimization seems to carry the least tangible value compared to implementation and test. However, in most cases the design imperfections and hidden bugs (technical debts in Scrum's term) make the software less maintainable and hard to understand and scale for the next rounds of new product development. In other worlds, in a mission-critical system a known bug should not be tolerated to be left out in the product for any duration of time.

On a different but related note, we should mention that in the eyes of the majority of engineers the documentation process fulfills no engineering purposes. That might be why Scrum gained such a rapid popularity among engineers. This is another backlash of blindfully abiding by the CPM and CPD rules for such a long time. We all know that most engineers lack stlar communications skills, so the unfriendly sparks as a result of friction between engineers and documents are inevitable. However, let's hope the everlasting desire of engineers to create things will fill this gap and overcome the friction. Therefore, Agile processes must not equate to document-less processes. The documentation process must be viewed as a tool of communication that establishes a technical definition dictionary to avoid false assumptions. The documentation is the glue that adheres everything in a development process. It is the grammar of the language spoken between various different departments involved in developing a product.

Looking back at the materials that have been presented thus far, there is a tremendous amount of evidence indicating that CPM has impacted project management in many good and fundamental ways. What is marked as a weakness for CPM is what exactly helped Agile methods to come into existence. That's the excessive documentations. The CPD, V-Model, and Scrum are all synthesized in the same laboratory or thought process. If it wasn't for the CPM process to record everything in a project, there wouldn't be any records for Agile methods to learn from the mistakes, identify the weaknesses, and come up with effective solutions. If we take away this powerful tool in our process we have effectively removed the means to improve the process.

Still today, if CPM is carried out the way it was meant to, it provides an impeccable method to develop products. But what was meant one day to be a tool became a goal, and project managers became happy with developing graphs, reports, and forecasts rather than carrying out the project in an effective way. From all the methods that have been discussed here, one common thing is a work breakdown structure; and a top-down approach to product development and project management is still alive and kicking.

Although Agile methods try to distance themselves from CPM they follow the same principles more or less. In Scrum, we might not see a general process but still we can witness that localized CPM and CPD are performing for the duration of a Sprint. Although Scrum claims to be an all-in framework for developing systems rather than only software, the lack of DFM, hardware-oriented processes, and minimal documentation make it difficult to make Scrum an inclusive tool for developing real-time systems as a whole. Remember that these systems are often used in time-critical applications such as mission-critical systems. However from Scrum comes a few noble ideas. Potentially shippable product is one of those original and unique concepts.

V-Model is unrealistic since for so long the developers go on designing an imaginary system without getting the feel of how it is really going to perform. Scrum breaks that habit and motivates the developers to create tangible work within a reasonable time, which creates a positive momentum and allows the project to move with a constant velocity. In addition to creating a steady pace for the project, the development team gets a sense of accomplishment during each iteration of a sprint.

In V-Model the design changes are hard to implement because this requires that various documents have to be updated simultaneously. It also poses a great challenge to the CPD process after the design freeze is imposed. This is why in the classical methods the changes are often not documented properly or not implemented at all, which poses even a greater challenge for troubleshooting at later times once the product is released, in addition to warranty challenges and liability commitments and even loss of lives.

Among all the items that DFM recommended to the developers, the most relevant item to a real-time system development is to implement a uniform method of development from concept to manufacturing and beyond on the field. This clearly shows that DFM supports Agile processes but the question is if the implemented Agile processes comply with DFM. Model-based design can be one of these tools that would flow easily throughout the entire development process.

We know the Scrum is there to replace CPD, but the real question is if Scrum can still create interfaces to interact with the antiquated and dominated existing management and financial establishments the way that CPD did. But let's look at this problem again. Neither core concept of CPD is outdated as it is how any logical process develops, nor does Scrum have all the answers to product development that could just drop in CPD's place and solve all the problems overnight. The solution might lie in a hybrid concept that creates a structured Scrum, which creates a project management position that is more involved than a Scrum master but also is more hands-on with the technical aspect of the system in dealing with real issues. Let's go back to the introduction of this book where we looked at the lessons learned from civil engineering. In a building construction, the project manager is also the system architect. Therefore let's combine these two positions in our real-time system development project into one and let's call our project manager a "Project Architect."

Bibliography

[1] Chang, Tien-Chien, Richard A Wysk, and Hsu-Pin Wang. *Computer-Aided Manufacturing* (2nd ed.). Upper Saddle River, NJ: Prentice Hall, 1998, pp. 596-598.

CHAPTER 3

Convergence of Management and Architecture

This chapter will present a perspective on the a project management process and a system architectural tool, which together create a complete and uniform framework for developing real-time systems across hardware and software platforms. We will review some powerful tools and methods that will empower the project managers to architect a system or system architects to manage a project. We want to bring together these two powerful positions, organically, into the organizational chart along with the rest of the development team. Performing this process and its unique tools, unlike other traditional methods, allows you to make only the product, and not the processes or the tools, at the center of the project. Along the way we will come across some more powerful tools that will differentiate this method of product development from other product development methodologies.

The requirement model is a classical method to establish function definitions in a systematic and hierarchical fashion. This is because, when the prophets of Agile methodology were busy in their advance laboratories to create wonderful Agile method, they seemed to forget to add some potion of old tricks to the mix. As a result the requirement model is not mentioned anywhere in their manifestos. But not to worry: the big boys in aviation and automotive industries know when it comes to acquiring certification from the government and other institutions, or when it comes to thriving for high-quality products where there are lives at stake, they need more than what an Agile system can offer. Since almost all embedded systems are designed to fulfill some type of critical-mission functionalities, utilizing a requirement model is absolutely imperative. A software flaw in a computer on, for example, a car traveling through a

© Mohsen Mirtalebi 2017
M. Mirtalebi, *Embedded Systems Architecture for Agile Development,*
https://doi.org/10.1007/978-1-4842-3051-0_3

winter storm, a wild ride in your local theme park, an airplane in midair, a smart phone making an emergency phone call, or in mission control room of a power plant, can lead to catastrophic outcomes.

However, it's been more than 20 years since Hatley and Pirbhai[1] introduced their version of the requirement model. Since then the landscape of product development has been revolutionized. The old method of paper and pencil kept in metal file cabinets full of drawings is long gone. The light-documented Agile processes are introduced and computers are leading the way on every aspect of the projects. However, the school of thought behind the requirement model still holds their true values. We will show how the old mindsets will still work marvellously in the new processes.

Convergence of Management and Architecture

The nature of real-time systems has changed from when they came to existence decades ago. The market is demanding smarter and more integrated systems. As a result the complexity of real-time systems has shifted from mechanical enclosures, packaging, and hardware to a new horizon we could have never envisioned several years ago, to firmware and software. Now we are expecting to fix anything with the software. Even the embedded system manufacturers think firmware should fill the functional gaps left behind by the hardware. This is because the stakeholders think the software is free, despite the fact they hire thousands of software engineers every year to develop them. But actually they might have a point. The cost of hardware development is now so high that the software development cost is easily overshadowed. But this trending software complexity, the lack of unified methods, and ever-changing face of technologies, have made the software development a bottleneck in the entire developmental process.

On the other hand, we know that software touches every aspect of the product development from concept to manufacturing, product diagnostics, and asset management. To have a consistent product development process and in accordance to proven DFM principals, we need to unify development tools and processes for all the major players in the project. One of these processes that we can consider is the requirement model process. Although Scrum is a power tool for developing PC-based software, it is not fully inclined toward a real-time system development, mainly because in the real-time systems, hardware has a much larger role than, for example, in a pure software project such as an inventory system design and implementation. However there should be a middle ground between Scrum and CPM for real-time system development.

As you might remember we have covered a summary of various topics that a project manager might come across in the process of real-time system development. What we have discussed so far was at an introductory level with a very brief history and applications of these topics to the extent that was beneficial to understanding the core idea of this book, which will be discussed in details later. The rest of this book will try to show you that documentation process in the requirement model is a major player in this game and it should be viewed as a powerful tool rather than a burden. Please note, although I have brought a detailed example in the last chapter, we intend to show **what has to be designed for a real-time system – not to show you how to design it**. In this process we start from identifying the common structures in the majority of real-time systems and then base our methods on these common and popular systems. At the end, we hope you feel confident that you have learned how these methods can apply to the common embedded applications; you can get creative and tailor them to fit your special applications.

A Requirement Model

The requirement phase used to be a major part of highly sensitive software development processes in aerospace and defense industries. As a result they were an integral part of their software life cycle. This is why there is a specific phase named requirements in CPD and also V-Model. The mission criticality of software and hardware of embedded systems demanded the creation of a requirements model not to fancy the stakeholders with complicated graphs. The requirements model is especially useful when a thorough definition of the system's inputs, outputs, and functions are needed. Although the modern Agile methods tend to claim they are all inclusive when it comes to software applications, in Scrum there is no specific mention of what if the system mission is so critical that it would roll over some of their principles. This is because Scrum likes to differentiate itself from CPM by being light on documentations and heavy on creating a value stream and productivity. Nevertheless, in reality, even in traditional developmental processes such as CPD, the process is anchored on requirements and documentations, and the documents are often either developed incorrectly or developed incomplete and never fully completed. Let's remember that the requirements are only a tool for a better design and ease of communication, not to show off our visual artistic talent.

In addition, documents are the proof of work done, act as legal records in courts, or used for acquiring certificates. Although the project managers can make this part of the project as fancy and extensive as they want to, for the sake of Agile methodologies we should consider an optimum point between extensive documentations or no documentations at all in real-time system development. For this reason our practical and precise requirement model must be centered around the main function of the product; and there is only one way to achieve that: to include an architectural model that comes from the heart of the product's features. To deal out all the product features, we must break down the product functionalities into modules and components that consequently will precisely define all the inputs and outputs to the system. Let's allow the product to define the inputs and outputs and not what we think the product needs. On that account, there is no difference between hardware and software as these two entities are united to develop one real-time system. So let's leave behind any prejudice toward hardware or software, focus on product function, and develop your requirement agnostics to hardware or software. By doing this, you will avoid unnecessary design constraints and will keep one in mind. By the time you get to design, implement, and test your functional modules, new doors and ideas have opened up.

An Architectural Template

As we discussed earlier, the software takes a few different forms on various phases of the development process. Many of these roles that software takes up to play are mainly supportive and not directly related to the main product functions. A massive chunk of total software created during the development is to address the hardware requirements especially to ensure its safe operation, which means in an embedded system, software and hardware tightly function together. Therefore they must act in a specific coordinated correlation. Some of these software-hardware functional correlations are rather obvious, especially when it comes to product function. That's why the hardware's software drivers are called firmware. In other words, the software will act as an integral part of the system. However, there are cases in which the correlation between the hardware and software is not as obvious and needs some attention. For example, as we discussed earlier in the software's reusability section, some software are widely used for hardware part qualification processes specifically at the concept stage, often at design stage, always at the manufacturing stage. and sometimes in field operations. The hardware qualification process is mostly software driven no matter what stage the product is at. Therefore in the embedded systems, the hardware-software relationship is always there whether it's evident to us or not. Therefore the software in embedded systems development is not a commodity we sell to the customers. With this in mind, an architectural model in a real-time system comprises both hardware and software architectural models at every stage of the product. Figure 3-1 depicts this concept.[1]

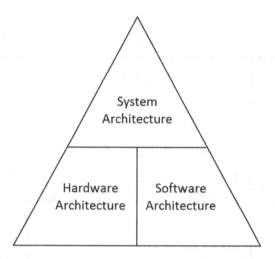

Figure 3-1. *An overall real-time system architecture*

As you can see the system architecture is comprised of hardware and software architecture, and the first step of development is to define how we can break down the system architecture into two separate but highly correlated architectures. However there is good and bad news for you regarding the system architecture and its breakdown structure. The bad news is, it might seem very easy to achieve a system division by having a T in the middle of a triangle, but in reality it can be a nightmare to assign product functionalities to either hardware or software units. The good news is that there is a proven systematic solution that helps us to break down this complexity into smaller and simpler steps. This good news is brought to you by the requirements model.

Hatley and Pirbhai [2] introduce an architectural template that works for almost all real-time systems. The template works for both hardware and software systems, which comprise Interface Processing, System Input Processing, System Output Processing, and Main Process and Control units (Figure 3-2). You don't have to strictly follow this template, but this is a simple and practical solution that can be scaled up or down depending on your application requirements. Although this might at the beginning look like a two-dimensional drawing, as we observed at the introduction section of this book it can, like a building's architectural drawing, contain many functional and physical layers.

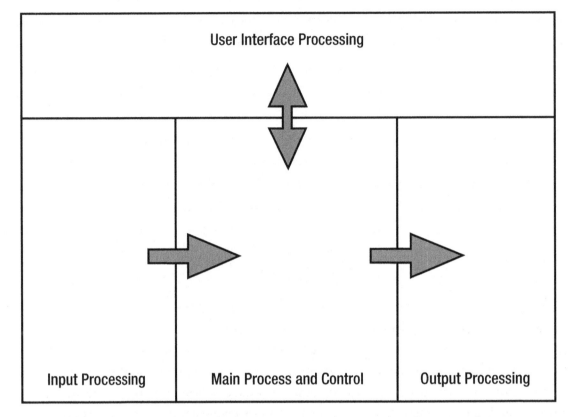

Figure 3-2. *An embedded system architecture with its main functional modules*

It shouldn't be hard to figure out that the template is modeled after our body: its sensory, mechanical, nervous systems, and so forth. We employ a series of sensory organs that receive data and control signals, process the signals, and reissue a multitude of other control and data signals. The brain contains the main process and control unit. However we don't have a user interface processing unit simply because we are a fully autonomous system. We don't take a user command to operate; therefore there is no need for a user-interface processing unit.

Hardware/Software Modules and Interfaces

As we've seen earlier, under the system architectural model, there are hardware and software modules that are often closely related. A requirement model must address both the hardware and software requirements. The requirements model also includes their interfaces with respect to hardware-hardware, software-software, and hardware-software interfaces and correlations. The interfaces are always the hot point and the causes of vast numbers of product failures. Often a module works perfectly by itself until it is made to interface with another module. Although the interfaces are the hot spots in design, implementation, and testing, if the development team rightly decides to consider developing two sets of requirements for both hardware and software under a single system requirement model, then the HP model is still able to help the engineers to visualize data and control flow. As we mentioned before, we are after **what has to be designed for a real-time system – not how to design it. The examples brought here are only to show you some specific use cases for the model.**

Please note some modules only handle data, control, or data and control. The Control signals tell software or hardware modules to come online and process their inputs in a certain fashion prescribed by the module's algorithm. For example, an input port of an analog to digital converter hardware (ADC) is triggered with a hardwire control signal that starts a hardware sampling process. Then again the ADC buffer is a piece of hardware whose readiness will trigger a software submodule to collect the data. As you can see for a simple data conversion task, there are some coordinated hardware and software actions along data and control signal flows. Both of these control and data flows need to be defined in a requirement document along their interdependencies. In another example, in a motor drive system, the inverter section is responsible to accept PWM control signals as input to control the gates of the IGBT switches in such a way that the input DC becomes an AC. The software is responsible to generate the PWM switching patterns in order to control the physical switches. Another example is in an automotive product where the cruise control module in a vehicle receives the control signal from the driver to activate the cruise control hardware and software submodules. Then both modules receive, process, and generate new rounds of data and control signals. This is to show how interconnected the hardware and software are in a real-time system. Although, as we've seen so far, in the embedded system product there is a fundamental correlation between hardware and software, but in reality these two development processes follow entirely different paths.

Product Life Cycle

For example, in a software development process, engineers follow various different models such as V or waterfall models. Ironically, under these traditional methods while a software life-cycle model such as V-Model represents the WBS of only the software part of the product, a CPD model wants to depict a more comprehensive image of the product development life cycle as a whole, which is not limited only to design and test but also gives a bigger picture regarding all the necessary steps to form a complete product, a wholesome hardware, and software development.

In spite of the fact that all the traditional product development processes point to the fact that there should be a unified process for both hardware and software development, unless the companies come up with their own creative solutions to glue these two different processes, currently there is no standard method to marry these two development processes under CPD.

In the meantime, in a real-time system, software carries the heaviest weight and complexity in the embedded system development. Then let's ask, wouldn't it be logical to expand one of the software developmental processes to cover both hardware and software development, considering we can tailor it so it meets all the product's demands? If so, then let me offer you the V-Model as a strong candidate for this choice. It's a prominent practice, it follows a logical process, and most importantly it's simple. However the V-Model heavily relies on two lengthy and costly processes: design and testing. But perhaps we can modify it so it can fit into modern developmental frameworks such as Agile while holding a defined form that is friendly to conservative developmental models such as CPD, which look at the product as a whole and not just segmented hardware and software units.

Product Breakdown Structure (PBS)

Product breakdown structure is similar to WBS in CPM. If we assume the product is also a work to be done, then WBS is the same as PBS. For the software and hardware breakdown structures, let's assume there are three levels to the product on each hardware and software platforms: systems, modules, and components. For the larger and more complex products we might need more layers such as units, submodules, and subcomponents; but for the sake of simplicity let's assume the mentioned three levels. For example, a vehicle is comprised of various systems including electrical and mechanical systems. Its electrical system might break down to monitoring and control modules and the monitoring module can be comprised of speed, fuel, and maintenance monitoring components. Each component then can break down to subcomponents and so forth until the amount of developmental work results in components that can be confined to the efforts of any **single developer per Sprint**. So if you think this process seems a lot like a combination of CPM, V-Model, and Scrum it's because it is but on a micro scale. The micro V-Model in a Scrum environment represents a micro

CPD development process that will be explained in more detail in later chapters. So for now, just keep in mind that this is the reason we are intending to modify the traditional V-Model. What is important is that, as we saw in the building architecture, the most intuitive and safe approach for creating a new product is the top-down method, which complies with the CPD process. The modified V-Model enables and keep us focused just to reach this very important architectural goal.

Product Development Team

If we accept that a combination of V-Model and CPD is feasible to implement, then based on DFM principals of unified processes and tools and Scrum's concept of "a potentially shippable product," a real-time system development team should be comprised of various multidisciplinary engineering, manufacturing, sales, and purchasing units. The entire team would be involved with the product from concept to deployment. Therefore there would be no wall to throw the design over. The project architect can expand or contract the roles of team members as s/he sees fit. For example, below is a sample of a possible functional team. These are not new functions in the development team, but the level of participation of these new team members is raised. In this somewhat new team dynamics, we have expanded the traditional definition of "developers," which used to be confined only to design engineers, to everyone involved in developing a new product.

- **Marketing Personnel**: Define the overall scope of the project and represent end-user expectations. In Scrum and CPD they are product owners and stakeholders respectively.

- **Research Engineers**: Receive feedback from the team for the part selections, practical manufacturing ideas, resolving design and implementation issues, resolving manufacturing test issues, etc.

- **Purchasing Personnel**: To identify and recommend parts, based on their availability, end-of-life status, logistics, and supply chain management, out/in-sourcing, delivery, and so forth.

- **Design Engineers**: Conventionally known as the developers. In a DFM-based team organization every team member is essential and is considered a developer. As a result everyone beside the design engineers will contribute directly to product throughout the development process.

- **Manufacturing Engineers**: Qualify parts, and recommend board material and layout for the printed circuit boards to ease the manufacturing, logistical processes, and improve the quality of products. The manufacturing engineering role impacts the product's final price directly.

Creating Requirements

Creating requirement documents is a tedious job for two reasons. First of all, most engineers like to jump right into the design and develop prototypes. Secondly, envisioning a complex system and laying down its details on paper seems a far-fetched idea at the beginning of the project when everything seems rather vague. However, these two reasons are exactly why we need to pay extra attention to the requirement development process. Jumping into any project without studying its requirements is guaranteed to prolong the project's time and increase the cost because it adds reworks to all development. Project complexities provide no excuse for the lack of requirements as these documents will break down the project complexities to smaller and more manageable portions. Documentation is the very reason the engineering profession exists.

Every Problem Is a Communication Problem

When Alexander Graham Bell developed the first phone line, he pioneered the communication theory. Years later with the development of the first computers, the information and control theories stemmed from this theory. Control and information theories as well as communication theory are widely used in the development of embedded systems. On the other hand, we know that interfacing hardware and software modules is either through communication lines, power lines, or both. To make this problem a bit simpler let's assume the power line is also a communication line where instead of messages, the electrical power is communicated. From my observation while serving in various industries, the majority of electrical failures in the embedded systems in the field are attributed to cables, connectors, and wire harnesses as well as EMI effects on PCBs.

On the other hand, based on my observation, in human interaction among the developers, miscommunication or lack of communication are blamed for the majority of product design flaws. Therefore, establishing clear and robust communication channels, whether in its technical or social form, on the product or among the team members is of grave importance.

In a DFM environment, the developer engineers have both internal and external customers. For example, the team that develops a control algorithm might have a client that includes a team of system developers who are in charge of programming the peripherals for sending and receiving data and control signals to and from the control firmware. The control firmware team is in charge of developing the core functionality of the product. The nature of communication between the control firmware and system firmware does not depend on the size of the company. In the smaller companies where the developers possess more T-shaped skill sets and put various hats on, the line between engineering roles are blurred, but this should not yield to blurring the line between responsibilities.

Any system architecture must distinguish separate product functionalities and to establish clear and robust communication among teams developing them, whether these teams are organized based on product modules or in the smaller companies where the teams share the responsibilities of developing various modules. Shared responsibilities do not dismiss the need to draw clear lines between various product functionalities and functional modules. Hence it is requiring establishing communication protocols among these functions in the team and also product modules. Bottom line: a product architecture should be agnostic about development teams also. It should only focus on how the product functions.

Consequently the control firmware team might have to face its data and control structures in a fashion that would comply with system communication protocols, database structures, and system timings. This might not be the case in all project or organizations, but the important idea is that at the requirement level, all data and dependencies among hardware and software modules, manufacturing processes, part purchasing, logistics, deliveries, and many other dependencies will be identified with enough details. We will come back to this topic again later when we discuss the system architectural template.

Unlike what's customary in many companies following the V-Model and CPD frameworks, we are not asking for an extensive and expensive requirements development process with various detailed documents, but we need at the minimum level, a system definition spelling out inputs, outputs, and functions within modules in a tabular format. For example let's assume a table of data on a hall element's temperature sensitivity, represented the curve characteristics (Figure 3-3) under a constant field of 300 Gauss (Figure 3-4).

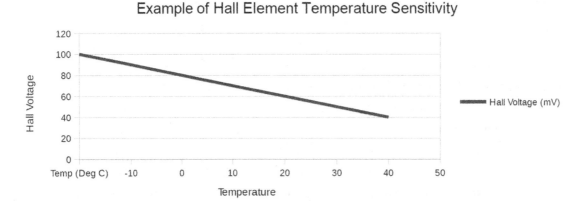

Figure 3-3. *A typical Hall element temperature dependency*

This means that this sensor under a relatively constant magnetic field of 300 gauss will demonstrate a gradual decrease on its output voltage as the temperature rises. To be able to manufacture a product that would linearly operate under temperature ranges, we must come up with a temperature compensation algorithm that would reside in the control firmware and would run at certain intervals.

One might ask why don't we just buy a part that can compensate the temperature right at the hardware level? The answer is because utilizing hardware to compensate the temperature effect is not economically justifiable. Additionally we have realized that we have a temperature sensor readily available for other purposes that we could also utilize for this purpose. A software component with the following requirement can be rendered to compensate for the temperature for a given magnetic field.

Whether we follow a V-Model or are in a freestyle developmental process such as Scrum, whether we are developing hardware or software components, we must define the requirements for this functionality followed with test procedures. Both V-Model and Scrum methodologies are strictly for software development; however the idea can apply to any other parts of a real-time system or all the phases of CPD. In Scrum, if developing the component was assigned to a developer for the duration of a Sprint then the test specification would be the same as acceptance criteria for this story. However the difference is that in Scrum there is no push for requirements.

Hall Element Temperature Compensation Software Component Requirement		
Component Inputs (x)	Component Outputs (y)	Description
1- Hall Element Temp (C) 2- Magnetic Field (Gauss)	1- Temperature Compensated Hall Voltage (mV)	$y1 = f(x1,x2)$ Note 1: Firmware team is responsible to derive the necessary equations. Note 2: Hall Voltage-Temperature Curve Temp (Deg C) Hall Voltage (mV) -10 100 0 90 10 80 20 70 30 60 40 50 50 40

Figure 3-4. *A Hall element's basic functional requirements*

Please note that in part, because of this requirement, raw hall sensing is carried out by the hardware; and the other part, temperature compensation, is performed by the software. Since we developed our requirement for this function we can now move on to test it. Based on the V-Model for every requirement there should be a test procedure to ensure the product meets the requirement. An example of a test spec for this module could be as the following in Figure 3-5.

Hall Element Temperature Compensation Software Component Test Spec		
Component Inputs (x)	Component Outputs (y)	Description
1- Apply product's temperature range to the component. 2- Apply a constant 300 Gauss Magnetic Field with a sweet spot of 2 sqrdmm area and 85% uniformity.	Temperature Compensated Hall Voltage should equates to a Constant Field of 300 Gauss on across temperature range with 2% error.	Regression testing in additional to functional testing so to make sure for a bounded input this software component is able to generate bounded output.

Figure 3-5. *Temperature compensation for a Hall element*

As you can see, we don't have to create a spectacular document to be called requirement and test specification document. Outlining the major parts of the functionality would be sufficient at the beginning. Later, you will see that you can add the requirement and test specs to the Model-Based Design models, all in one place. The rest of the spec will be detailed out as the project progresses. However, to achieve a cohesive method for requirements modeling development, we need to come up with a process that can be applied to any project and stays applicable throughout the process. The first step in creating a cohesive process is to analyze the marketing requirements. Again by requirements here, we mean developing a requirement specs in its traditional and popular form known as a Marketing Requirements Document (MRD).

Marketing Requirements Document (MRD)

Writing a good marketing requirements document is a talent that is rare. Technically the marketing people are the sole owners of the new products. However in technology sectors, often a product under development is an orphan. It seems because of uncertainties no one wants to take ownership of the product. A product with a clear owner will demonstrate magnificent attributes and achieve many goals such as shorter time-to-market time, smaller development costs, larger profit margins, and higher levels of customer satisfaction. If the marketing people were doing a good job of representing the customers, we would be facing a totally different world, perhaps with less problems and waste.

Nevertheless, discussing the shortcomings of the technology management is not in the scope of this book. Instead we try to steer away the development away from these problems by creating a new position called project architect, which is able to convert partial customer requirements to detailed design documents focusing in on a single goal of creating a robust new product. You might ask why we introduced this new position? How this position combining project management and product architecture jobs can contribute to developing a robust product? Can a product architect control project time, quality, and cost? The answer is yes. As we saw in the construction example in the earlier chapters, a robust product is born out of knowledge about the product requirements, functionalities, and limitations. An organized development starting with a robust requirements definition and clear architectural outlines yields to a strong product that is sought after by the customers.

Normally marketing documents explain customer's expectations from the product in terms of temperature range, the effect of environment on the product, user interfaces, voltage and current operating ranges, power consumption, modes of operations, speed, efficiency, and other conditions. They also might include regulatory and certifications requirements, patent issues and in some cases product test specifications. If the MRD lacks any of the mentioned items then it is the development teams' responsibility to expand these documents in details.

Since the marketing requirement document looks at the product from the customer's perspective, it can serve as a requirement document for the architectural phase of the product development. Although the marketing requirement can come very close to product architectural design, it is not an architectural document. To make MRD a design document, developers must identify the major software and hardware modules of the real-time system.

Conceptual Design

After developing the preliminary architectural document and identifying the major parts of our real-time system, we need to develop the prototypes. Prototyping is a hot topic among developers whether they come from CPD or Agile frameworks. In CPD, concept development comes before architecture. This is because a project is handled like a business plan. The program managers must convince the stakeholders that the initial concept of the product is sound and the project is economically feasible in order to get the necessary funding.

However in Agile or many other derivatives of it such as Scrum, the prototyping is not mentioned. Many developers, especially the ones developing embedded systems, have attempted to fit the concept development into an acceptable format for Scrum. Sprint zero or in some cases called Sprint minus one is a result of that attempt. However the sprint zero is not an official Scrum concept since it has an open-ended duration and a mixed backlog of items including team organization, logistics, etc., which seem to be a hodgepodge of odds and ends that won't fit in the normal Scrum setting.

Prototyping can be viewed from various perspectives with various levels of complexity in design and cost. However the type of prototyping we intend to picture here is the proof-of-concept type of demonstration to the project stakeholders for founding purposes while it is on its path to become a full-featured product. The prototype can be entirely a simulation model, a complete working concept, or anything in between.

Depending on the stakeholders' level of technical inclination and general reception of the idea, the project architect can create a sample of a product.

All in all, in the spirit of avoiding waste generation we do not take the concept of development to be a trivial matter. There are many hours of careful thoughts, years of experience, and many ingenious ideas have put into work to create a prototype. Whether your ideas pass the concept phase or get rejected by the financial watchdogs, the components and knowledge it carries will not go away. If your idea is accepted by the stakeholders, you can transform your prototype into a product and if it's rejected it can fuel another project idea. Therefore the proof of concept is the first potentially shippable product of the project in a Scrum frame of work. It is also strongly recommended that the concept prototype architecturally represents the entire system with all its layers. This is because the DFM and Agile are constantly forcing us to think "Product" throughout the development process. A prototype is not a complete product, but it should represent all the major product modules in one form or another.

Therefore a prototype cannot be destroyed; rather, it transforms from one form to another. The ideas discussed in this book will allow you to see what needs to be done to preserve the invaluable knowledge you put into countless hours of your prototyping activities and what to recycle in order to fuel the entire product development process.

Simulated Prototyping

As there are no two equal types of products, even in the same class and in the same company, the new products are always unique; therefore you can't use a prototype of a legacy product to serve as a prototype for a new product. You shouldn't even use a legacy product to work as a prototype for a new product. This is because each design is unique even though the differences might seem minimal. By introducing an old product to a new design, you are unwillingly inviting all the unnecessary legacy design constraints and that's the worst thing that can happen to a design process at its infancy. You can use part of a legacy product in a prototype or the whole legacy product in part of a prototype, but never base your new design on an old product because in the age of computers you have a lot more other sound options at your disposal.

Some prototypes in the real-time systems are pure software based, some pure hardware, and a lot of them are a combination of both. Since the design at the concept level is mostly dealing with the new ideas, inventions, groundbreaking concepts, and so forth, simulation models are very important. These models not only are used for concept proofing but also for establishing design benchmarks that could be carried out throughout the entire CPD or Scrum processes even when the product is launched and is being used in the field. The most popular example of the design benchmark that is being carried over to the field is the diagnostic features for products such as frequency and step responses, self-calibration routines, auto-tuning, etc., which can be performed occasionally or systematically in forms of electrical or mechanical tests at a customer's fingertip.

Rapid Prototyping

By using Model-Based Design (MBD) tools, one can generate very quick conceptual results that can be implemented on the hardware. Depending on the availability of the hardware prototypes there will be different prototyping approaches.

Model in the Loop (MIL)

In MBD, a part of the system is represented and simulated in conjunction with the rest of the existing system whether it is only comprises hardware, software, or both.

- **Model in a hardware loop**: There are many MBD tool vendors who can provide you with hardware adapters that can allow you to interface your system hardware with your model or allow your model to be downloaded on their hardware, and then it will be interfaced with another hardware that poses as plant hardware. This means your model in its original graphical format can get in the hardware loop and be tested for its performance. As we mentioned, the hardware can be a plant model that is being simulated on another autonomous simulation system or an actual real-time system hardware. In Figure 3-6, you can build your control model in a host computer in a non-real-time environment then download it to a custom hardware that can accept your model as is. The model will be compiled to another programming language or possibly directly into machine language. The custom hardware then would act as your ideal target processor that you are planning to manufacture. Custom hardware then would be interfaced with a power module, for example, IGBT switches and through that you can test your new control scheme by translating electrical power to force or energy, in this case, possibly an electromechanical system such as a motor.

- **Model in a software loop**: If we omit the plant hardware and power
  module in Figure 3-6 and instead feed back the control signals
  from the input of the power module to enter the host computer and
  create a software test harness in the host computer with pass and
  fail criteria, then we are able to test our model. Another alternative is
  to create our model in a real-time simulator and create the software
  test harnesses in the same environment. In this case our model to be
  simulated and tested is called Unit Under Test (UUT) and the rest of
  real-time system surrounding our models is be considered as the test
  harness. In this case a form of software is interacting with another
  form of software in order for evaluation and benchmarking purposes.

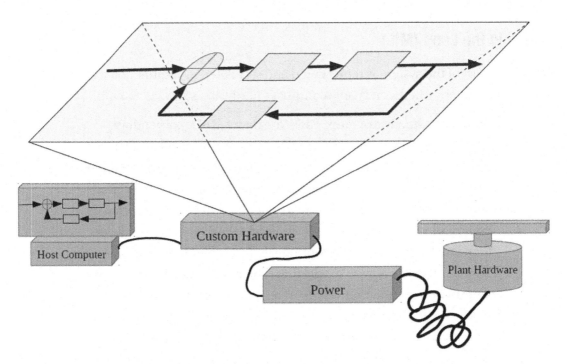

Figure 3-6. *Model in the loop basic topology*

Software in the Loop (SIL)

The MBD tool vendors also can provide you with another feature that would allow
you to generate code from a model in C, C++, or some other different programming
languages, depending on their integrated development environment (IED). The model
then automatically generates the code that can be used in hardware and software loops

similar to what we described in the MIL method. In this case we use a program often in a textual form to interact with the rest of the system and not a model, which in MIL was represented in a graphical format. We normally utilize SIL when the models have passed the POC stage. The SIL is a step closer to actual product simulation because it's the code in the product that eventually interacts with the real world.

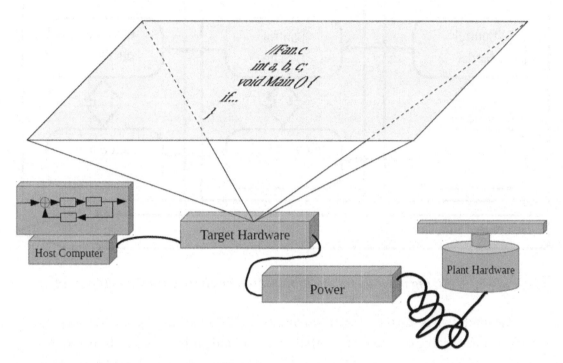

Figure 3-7. *Basic software in-the-loop topology*

Hardware in the Loop (HIL)

The last and most important part of testing your software is to download it into the target hardware. By this time, hopefully your actual hardware is developed; otherwise your software can be downloaded into an evaluation board that utilizes the same microprocessor as the final product. Then the target can be either used in another hardware loop or in a pure simulated environment. There will be numerous possibilities to mix and match hardware with software. For example, if your product is a new DC-DC converter that is being used in a power system project, the load or plant can be a piece of software that simulates a power grid in real time via a simulator. Figure 3-8 depicts a summary of how MIL, SIL, and HIL are positioned with respect to the rest of the system.

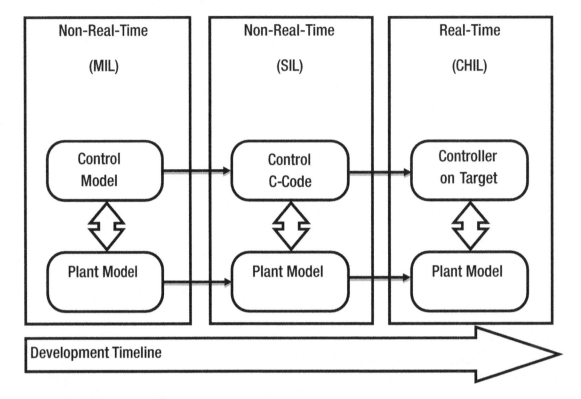

Figure 3-8. *Utilizing various in-the-loop topologies in product development*

Concept design is the most important phase of CPD in terms of proof of concept; therefore it will set the course for the other phases of the project. As we discussed before any hardware and software development, especially at the HIL stage, can be recycled and scaled for any other phases of CPD.

Consequently a well-designed HIL system can be the first potentially shippable product. Let's reaffirm that at this stage the product is not complete, it is not cost effective, safe, or fully featured; but by the definition it carries the core functionality of the end product, therefore it is potentially shippable. This is very important to treat the concept prototype as a product because for the rest of the project, its parts and modules slowly will evolve and be replaced with safer, more cost-effective, and fully featured parts and modules.

There are many ways to do the simulation and prototyping in a cost-effective way without compromising the integrity of the scientific efforts. It is not important how we name the proof-of-concept phase, whether we insert it in the sprint zero or we put it in the backlog as part of a potentially shippable product as long as its creation does not constitute discontinuity in scope, method, or product. The goal is to recycle 100% of everything happening in this phase for other phases of product development.

Also in Figure 3-8 you can see a few other names and approaches in prototyping. As you can see the product/prototype starts as pure simulation and as the project progresses, scope of the product is more defined and risks are lowered as the product becomes more and more realized in a hardware form.

Proof of Concept

The proof of concept (POC) is part of any project that has ever been done successfully or has failed miserably, from a home remodeling project to changing a spare tire. The sequence you review in your mind before chaining the tire is technically your prototype. A POC can be in any format from a drawing on a napkin, computer simulations, or a full-fledged hardware prototype to an idea formed in your mind. Obviously the more an idea is developed and materialized, the higher its rate of success will be. For a real-time system a napkin note might get people to listen to your idea but will not get you a bank loan.

Furthermore to prove the concept, one must test the concept first. So building a cosmetic form of hardware for show-and-tell purposes is not enough; it must also be able to perform some functions. These functions might in part look like test routines. For example, *function_1* is to turn the green LED on after the pushbutton_1 is pressed and released within a second. This is to visually confirm the *function_1* works. However it also verifies that all the system components from software to hardware are functioning correctly.

Imagine a product is on its developmental path moving from one department to another: to a research engineer the test routine is to verify that the concept works; to a hardware and/or software engineer the same routine can be utilized and be called an engineering test to verify the hardware and software modules function per design; and to a manufacturing engineer it is a test with pass-fail criteria at the end of the manufacturing line. As you can see even testing methods, tools, hardware, and software can be recycled, duplicated, or scaled to be used in other departments.

Architecture Design

As we discussed before any real-time system has at least one architectural layer that includes software and hardware. Modules are the next layer in a system architecture and they are the main building blocks. A real-time system architecture has a minimum of four modules: User Interface Processing, System Input Processing, System Output Processing, and Main Process and Control units. Let's assume our real-time system is so simple that each module can run with one hardware or software component. Software and hardware components are the simplest form of a module. A collection of similar components make up a module. These compartmentalized components are simple enough that developers can design and implement them in one Sprint, one component per developer per single Sprint. Figure 3-9 would be one of the representations of a real-time system in the simplest form.

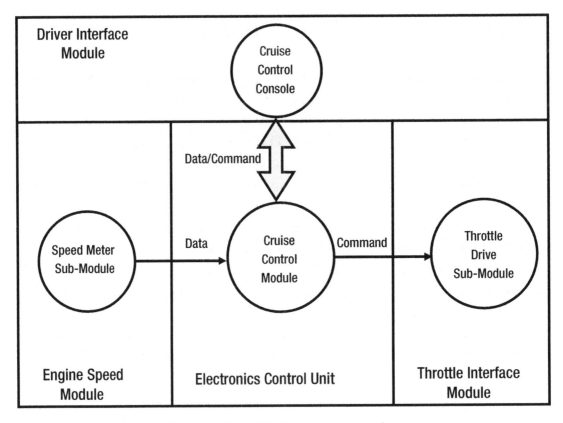

Figure 3-9. *System architecture for vehicle cruise control*

Please note that at the prototype level any of these modules and components can be substituted with the final released hardware, or software or can be replaced with component prototypes or be fully simulated with MIL, SIL, or HIL methods. It is up to the team to decide how to assemble these hardware and software parts depending on the part availability. However when the parts are assembled at the system level, a series of tests are required. If the system passes all the tests the product is pronounced a **potentially shippable product**. In a later chapter we will discuss what types of tests are at your disposal to qualify the prototypes.

Module Design

According to the requirement model and based on top-down architectural approach, the next step in our development is module design. The largest modules in our architectural template are the Data Processing and Control Modules. These two super-modules constitute the entire process and control unit for every embedded system application even though when you think your control is purely control based. This is because control algorithms relay heavily on input/output data processing more so in a real-time systems, which normally demand a timely stream of data. Therefore the architectural model that was introduced earlier would be as in Figure 3-10.

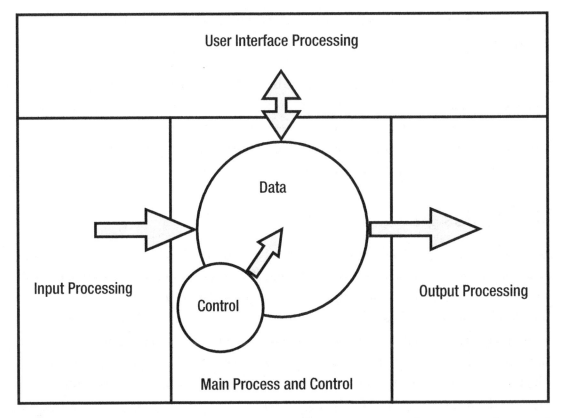

Figure 3-10. *Functional constraints in a real-time system with respect to data and control flow*

As you can see later, these two modules will later become two layers called data and control layers in the overall system structure. The data and control layers can have their own architectural layout in the larger and more complex products. Normally the databases and computational operations are placed on data layer, while operating systems and logical operations are placed on the control layer.

As shown in Figure 3-10, the connection between control and data processing units is shown with bold lines. This is because a control signal is discrete rather than being a constant stream of data. Therefore we are distinguishing between data and control signals. This is also true in the hardware layer as control signals/buses are normally different from communications/data streams and buses. For now think of control signals as triggering mechanisms to signal a hardware or software module to do something with the data. We will get into a more insightful analysis of these two grand functionalities when we discuss the component design.

What Constitutes a Module?

As a reminder, a module is a section of a functional architecture that performs a very specific function. The developers encapsulate functions in modules so as to increase the readability, maintainability, scalability, and the reusability of their programs or hardware. The software engineers seem to have a better handle of defining what a module is and how it should look like as in hardware due to a constant technology change and part obsolescence; modularity has some limitations: as a result the hardware engineers are extra careful when it comes to grouping components with similar functionalities. There are many ways to identify or structure a module but discussing this topic further is beyond the scope of this book.

Control and Data in Model-Based Design (MBD)

In model-based design, think of control modules as modules with logical operations and data modules as modules that contain mostly arithmetic and algebraic operations even though they calculate control gains. This is because they provide a constant stream of data (here in this example they are control data).

The control modules carry values on demand based on reaching threshold, max and min limits, or any logical combinations as a result of users or other modules' commands, for example, the commands from the operating system. Some powerful software packages such as Simulink(R) have two definition for different signals that can be used as "control" and "data" signals, for example, Simulink's designated "parameters" and "signals" can be used for control and data signals respectively.

Parameters are software variables that carry Boolean or constant values for some period of time but they are time invariant, meaning for a duration of time their values are held constant. On the other hand the data through the "signals" change in time for every instant of time. They are time-variant variables. Please see Figure 3-11.

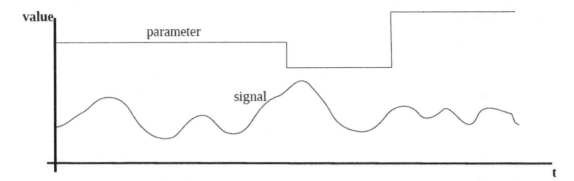

Figure 3-11. *Time-series representation of signal and parameter*

Now that we got the big picture of a real-time system design in terms of its architecture and major modules, we can discuss the most important part of it, the "component design" in greater detail. We do this because the components of a real-time system, whether hardware or software, are the most basic building blocks of the entire system.

Component Design and Product Breakdown Structure (PBS)

The components are the building blocks of a real-time system but to decompose the system into its building blocks requires following a systematic method.

Identifying a Component

- First decomposition rule: From when you decide to decompose an architectural model to its modules until when you decompose modules to its components, have the 7±2 in mind. An architectural model, modules, and submodules or any other parent module should contain a maximum of 9 and minimum of 5 modules. Anything less or more makes the design too simple or too crowded; hence it makes it hard to redesign, scale, or maintain. Remember that we want to welcome future changes, which cannot be avoided as the development moves ahead.

- You decompose the modules into submodules and components until you reach a unit of workload that is comparable to what is called "task" in WBS. Which means it's a workload that consists of a product component that can be performed by a single person (Task Component).

86

- The task-component should be sized to be performed in one unit of project time. This unit of time is comparable to what is called a "Sprint" in Scrum.

- The task-component would perform a single function (or feature in a Scrum term) of the system you intend to design.

- The decomposition should be uniform. Do not design modules that carry many submodules and then some that include too few of them.

- The decomposition should be performed one level at a time. Unlike Scrum, which offers no structure, the method we discuss here requires you to develop all the modules on the same functional level and complexity. Then you can move to the next level of which submodules or components reside.

- If you reach the component level too early for one submodule while other ones require additional levels to detail out the functionality, you should not worry. The goal here is to uniformly reach the component level. Later on you can reshuffle all these. Let's just focus on producing a feasible PBS while the team develops a good understanding about the system.

- Producing tangible results starts when there are enough details in hand that would allow us to draw some lines in the sand with respect to the functional responsibilities of the team members. In other words, the first sprint starts when there are enough task components in the backlog queue. Otherwise you are still in the per-first sprint stage. This is comparable to "Sprint Zero" in Scrum.

- Try to group modules with similar functionalities.

- Have a free mind. Don't box up the ideas. Try to avoid any constraints, logical or physical, until it's time to implement the design for each level of the architecture.

- If a module consists of only one submodule, either it must be combined with its parent module, or it is partially defined and needs to be expanded.

- Modules that carry he word "and" in their titles must be decomposed to two submodules. A "data management and system diagnostics" module consists of two submodules, "data management" and "system diagnostics."

- If you can't come up with a name for a module then it needs to be defined better and decomposed to more modules.

- Avoid creating partially defined modules, submodules, and components. Before moving on to the lower level you need to finish defining this one.

- Initially create the modules and components in their simplest form without deviating from its main functionality. An abstract functionality of a module with well-defined inputs and outputs is much better than detailed functional realization and partial input/output definitions.

- Remember there is no silver bullet in this process. It requires many iterations of inspect-adapt cycles. This is the part that carries the heaviest weight of the project in terms of development efforts, but it saves you much time at implementation, optimization, and deployment with minimum waste, which also guarantees a product with significant values in quality.

- The decomposition process is a brainstorming process and unlike WBS in CPM where it is only performed by the project manager, the best results are achieved in the context of a **functional team**.

- If the real-time system development processes were repeatable, the project managers could carry lessons learned, work and time studies, and work standardizations from one real-time system project to another. However, as most of us know, every technology-based project is unique due to parts, architecture, and methods obsolescence that occurs more frequently than it deems necessary.

Summary

No matter how you look at it, from CPM, Scrum, or V-Model perspectives, creating a work breakdown structure, backlog items, or V-Model hierarchy, is the foundation of the project. If we break down the project in such a way that we can follow the product function while creating tasks, we can achieve a unit of product that is the same as a unit of work. We'd like to call this unit a task component. The next chapter will explain how PBS and requirement models are closely related to each other.

Scrum, like any modernist movement, comes in response to the sluggishness of traditional methods, mainly the CPM methods. However the majority of the supporting organizations of the modern projects are still acting as nothing is changed and try to understand and analyze the projects based on traditional methods. After introduction of the Agile methods the developers like to conduct the project in an Agile way while the financial sectors like to track the projects down in traditional methods. On the other hand, methods such as CPD have a natural and structured flow to them that make them easy to understand and to track them down. In addition, the majority of embedded systems need to be certified by the organizations by which a structured development process is mandated. The new method would combine the Scrum process with planning sessions of V-Model and CPD in addition to some modern tools such as MBD and the requirement model to achieve PBS.

One of the most important shortcomings in Scrum comes right at the beginning of the project when it is the most critical time in the project. In the CPD process the concept phase is the first phase of the project when at the end the stakeholder will decide to whether allow the project to continue or not. Scrum has a philosophical contradiction when it comes to prototypes. Since a prototype is not a product, Scrum cannot decide whether to treat it as a product release or not. Some decide to treat it as a product release while they know that at the end there might not a product to release. Some would put it in their unofficial sprint zero phase. Either way, in Agile, prototyping efforts are vague and often defeat their own purpose to be a discovery tool than to be a project goal.

In the meantime the modern time has brought us some modern tools for product development. The MBD tools are such a powerful tools that if they are utilized properly the product requirement, design, and test phases can be lumped into one phase, shortening the time to market and cutting significant implementation and deployment costs.

Bibliography

[1] Hatley, Derek J., and Imtiaz A. Pirbhai. *Strategies for Real-Time System Specifications.* New York: Dorset House Publishing Co. Inc., 1988, p. 274.

[2] Ibid., p. 195.

CHAPTER 4

Requirements Model

Based on Hatley and Pirbhai [1], the foundation of any real-time system requirements model is its process and control models. As we discussed before, process normally refers to data handling, whether internal or external, and control refers to control schemes and signals as the gatekeeper of the data. Although Hatley and Pirbhai's (HP) method of developing relies heavily on paper-based documentations, its spirit is timeless as their logic can apply to any real-time system. Since the documentation process for HP method is obsolete, what will come in this chapter is only a skimmed summary. If the reader decides to dig deeper into the method, s/he can obviously consult with their book that is referenced at the end of this chapter and throughout this book. What we cover in this chapter will be mainly focused on HP's decomposition initiatives and function definition methods. The reason I mention HP method here is because it has a proven track record in aerospace and automotive industries in which embedded system efficiency and safety are of paramount importance.

Process and Control Requirements Model

Based on a general agreement and wider common concession in the engineering world, whether in the hardware or software environment, the requirement phase is a stage before design. It's where the knowledge of various engineering disciplines comes together to define the functionalities of the system. It does not lay out the details of the design, but it requires the product modules and the development processes to be defined by their functions and tasks respectively. At the top of the V-Model or at the very initial stages of CPD comes the marketing requirements document (MRD). For example, the marketing requires the product to function in a specific temperature, voltage, current, and pressure ranges. It might also require the finished product to acquire some international compliance certificates. The marketing requirement is not a process to conceptualize the product concept nor to materialize the end product. It only gives the

© Mohsen Mirtalebi 2017
M. Mirtalebi, *Embedded Systems Architecture for Agile Development*,
https://doi.org/10.1007/978-1-4842-3051-0_4

development engineers an initial boost to ignite the development processes and set some viewpoints to let the developers start decomposing the high-level requirements to the low-level engineering specs.

Context Diagrams

Each process and control model starts with a context diagram. You can think of a context diagram as an architectural level of PBS that has been extracted from the marketing requirements document and purely focuses on the functional aspect of the product regardless of how it would be designed and implemented. It's the most abstract document that explains how the product will function in the hands of customers. The Data Context Diagram and Control Context Diagram are the special cases of data and control flow diagrams (which will be explained later) but differ from other flow diagrams in which their main distinction is that they provide an interface with the external environment for your real-time system. Imagine a typical real-time system with a user interface to receive set point values, commands, and control signals where it also displays the system parametric status via some visual means to the user. Meanwhile, the central processing unit receives sensor values where some defined algorithms process the values and generate new sets of data and/or commands to other functional parts of the system.

As you can see in Figure 4-1, the entire real-time system is manifested in a very simple diagram that reflects only a limited functional aspect of the marketing requirements from the customer's standpoint. Evidently, the customer's view of the product is not necessarily as complicated as how the system developers view the product. However, you can have a state-of-the-art control algorithm in your system, but if the product does not function the way the customer wants it to, then you have failed. Sometimes just a word such as safety in MRD can completely change your development and eventually your product. Therefore, capturing all the requirement items one by one is vital. Ironically, a lot of time the MRD does not include everything in it. The consequential requirements are the ones generated from interacting requirement items in MRD. The developers are responsible for discovering, extending, and expanding the consequential requirements. Therefore, the safest way to capture all the requirements is to follow a systematic approach. The requirements model is the approach that is specifically designed for embedded systems development.

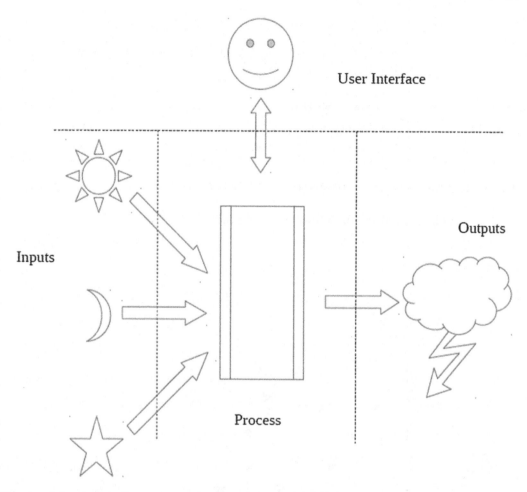

Figure 4-1. *A simple representation of an embedded system in the eyes of a customer*

Based on HP's method, after breaking down the system into major functional sections, we need to focus on each functionality to break them down into their simplest functional components. In Figure 4-2 the DCD and CCD contents are compared so you can have a better understanding of what purpose each one of them serves. The first-tier DCD and CCD correspond directly to the system architecture. As you might recall, a simplified system architecture has four main major functional modules: User Interface, Input, Output and process, and control units. Therefore, the DCD and CCD would correspond to the four modules. If you decide to have different sets of module with different naming, then you have to list your modules in the DCD and CCD. Consequently, the list of modules in Figure 4-2 corresponds to our modules stated in our architecture template.

Data Context Diagram Contents		Control Context Diagram Contents	
User Interface Data	Displaying Data and Receiving Set Point Values	User Interface Control	Displaying Status and Receiving Commands
		Input Control Signal	Receiving Fault Signal
Input Data	Reading Sensor Data	Output Control Signal	Sending Out Commands
Output Data	Sending Out Data		
Process Unit	Data Analysis	Control Unit	Control Processing

Figure 4-2. *DCD and CCD comparison in a requirement model*

Figure 4-3 illustrates the major architectural units of our system.

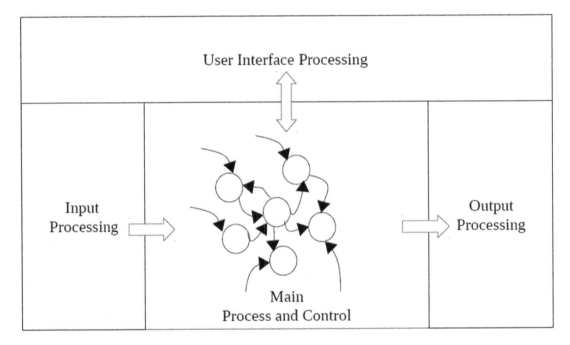

Figure 4-3. *Submodules in the grand view of system architecture*

Now by looking at Figure 4-3 and comparing it with Figure 4-2 of Context Diagrams, you can see how the context diagrams are positioned with respect to the architectural template of the system. The circles inside of Main Process and Control Unit are the representation of data and control flow for Main Process and Control module. To avoid crowding this diagram, I did not include submodules and components in the other three main modules; otherwise in reality all these four main modules are comprised of many submodules and components.

Flow Diagrams

If we consider the DCD and CCD as the product definition at the top tier of our architectural level, the flow diagrams are the same diagrams but at the levels blow. The difference between those diagrams and these is that there is only one set of DCD and CCD that describes the product requirement in abstract, and as the product gradually moves to the lower levels by decomposing the modules to submodules and components, more details are introduced and represented by the flow diagrams. There are two types of flow diagrams: Data Flow Diagram(DFD) and Control Flow Diagram (CFD).

Let's assume that our architectural template shown in Figure 4-3 is for a hardware counter product. Each circle in the DFD could denote a subfunction of the counter, for example, to carry out a synchronous/asynchronous, acceding/descending, absolute/relative operations and so forth based on the requirements stated in the MRD. Then the CFD would describe the control functionalities, for example, what the modules do or flag what fault if there is an overflow event.

There will be many iterations of hierarchical DFD and CFD with parent-child relationships that would create eventually a network of all circles and arrows describing all the product's functions. As illustrated in Figure 4-4, the DFDs and CFDs look similar visually but they carry different functionalities. Figure 4-5 shows how DCD will be broken down to DFDs passing through various stages of decomposition. Please note each circle indicates a functionality and each arrow is the flow: in this case data flow; also in the last stage I chose to encapsulate a control function as a reminder that control functions are not necessarily should put in the control modules. Many control modules and components submerge in the sea of data.

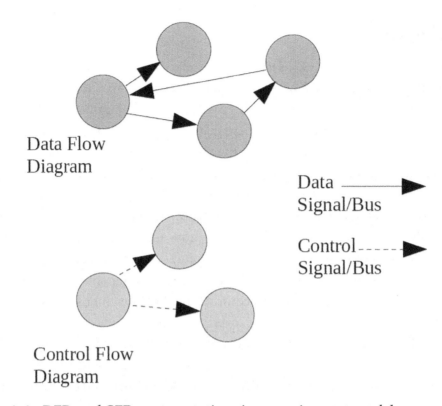

Data Flow
Diagram

Data ⸺▶
Signal/Bus

Control⤏▶
Signal/Bus

Control Flow
Diagram

Figure 4-4. *DFD and CFD representations in a requirement model*

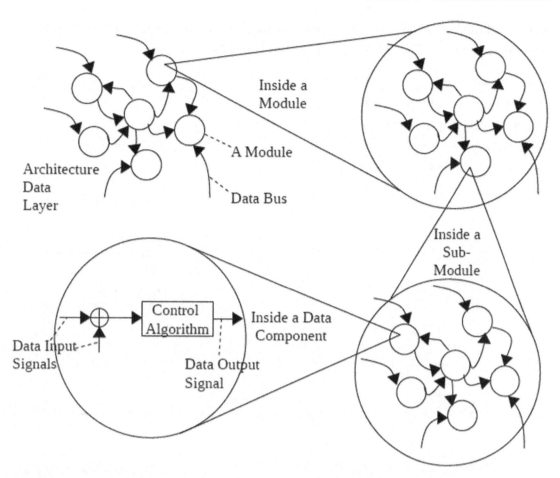

Figure 4-5. *The WBS in action, a top-down view of a system's data-related functionalities*

Process and Control Specification (PSPEC, CSPEC)

The PSPEC and CSPEC are developed when the work of decomposing flow diagrams through DFDs and CFDs are done. These two documents, PSPEC and CSPEC, show the functionality of each component and the relationships among them for the entire project where it leaves less to no ambiguity about the functionality, inputs, and outputs of a component. Hatley and Pirbhai [1] provide a useful graphical overview of data and control work breakdown structure. Figure 4-6 is a graph summarizing documents involving this process. There are various forms to express the PSPEC and CSPECs; one is structured English or Pseudo-Codes, or mathematical formulas, logical relationships, or a combination of all. The following is an example of a Pseudo-Code:

```
Measure Motion:
For each pulse of shaft rotation:
add 1 to 'Distance Count'
then set:
'Distance' = 'Distance Count'/'Mile Count'...
```

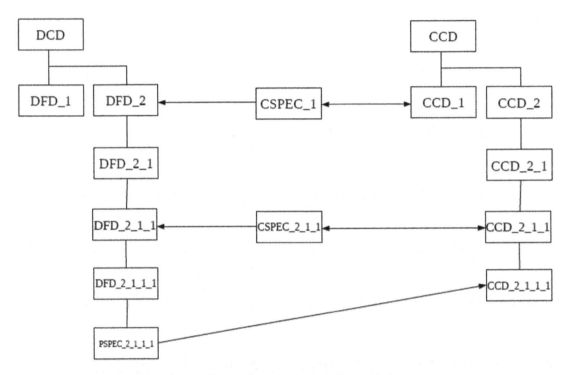

Figure 4-6. *The relationship between PSPEC and CSPEC*

Figure 4-6 gives an overview of the position and relationship of PSPECs and CSPECs with respect to the rest of our architecture. In simple words, PSEPC defines the functionality of a component and only components, not the modules or submodules. CSPEC defines the relationship between control and data flow in our architecture, whether at the component or module level, wherever they occur. Since control has a special vitality to the embedded systems it matters to define them through CSPEC documents at any level of architecture. On the other hand, we are not required to define the data at all levels of architecture because the data organization can change at any time depending on new discoveries in the development. This gives us flexibility on our data side while keeping the integrity of the functions. Therefore, it is safe to assume that PSPECs and CSPECs document the product function in both control and data domains. Please remember this diagram, as it shows how data and control functionalities of the same product stem from the same architectural ground but follow two different paths of growth.

The Requirements Dictionary

Based on Hatley and Pirbhai [1], the requirements dictionary is the most important part of the requirements model. This is because the dictionary defines the data and control functionalities of the hardware and software layers. It groups and organizes control and data functions alike, and identifies the sources and destinations of the data and control signals. This is like having to define all the I/O's to and from a software or hardware functions and to verify the scales, type, unit, limits, and dependencies on every single input and output signals. Since there are two types of signals, Data and Control, there will be two classes of I/O definitions: Continuous and Discrete.

The examples in Figure 4-7 are arbitrary just to portray that you can define the signals in any format and shape that fits your application. The goal here is to define all I/Os thoroughly in a universal fashion. These definitions are very important as they come in handy for the duration of the development and thereafter for years to come.

Continuous Signal Definitions					
I/O Name	Definition	Attributes			
		Units	Range	Resolution	Rate
Baro Alt	Barometric Altitude	Feet	0-70,000	1	1 Per 100 milsec
Shaft Rotation	Angular Rotation of Drive Shaft	Rad/Sec	0-20,000	-1	On Demand

Discrete Signal Definitions				
I/O Name	Definition	Attributes		
		No. of Values	Value Names	Rate
In Air	Wheels off ground	2	On, Off	1 Per 500 milsec
Flight Phase	Phase of vertical flight profile	4	Takeoff, Climb, Cruise, Descent	1 Per 200 milsec

Figure 4-7. *How to define parameters and signals in terms of continuous and discrete signals*

Timing Specifications

If you remember, at the beginning of this book, in the WBS section we asked you not to limit yourself by applying resource constraints on functional specifications. One of these constraints is the timing. Since in a real-time system, time is a very valuable and scarce resource, we must put a special emphasis on managing this resource. Once the requirements model is completed and all of the PSPEC and CSPECs are ready, the timing constraint must apply to each function. The next step would be to identify the frequency of execution of each function and tabulate this process. This is solely at a designer's discretion on what timing to be assigned to each function. The designer can pick an entire module to be executed at a certain rate or decide to customize the execution by the components. Figure 4-8 is only an example of a control scheme for a mechanical system.

External Input Signal	Event	External Output Signal	Event	Response Time
Shaft Encoder Value	Encoder Reader	Speed Feedback On LCD	Scaling	500 uSec max
Shaft Encoder Value	Speed Change	Throttle Position	Calculate the Change	1 Sec max
Resume Speed	Resume Speed,Check if it is not in top gear or breaking	Throttle Position	Return to Desired Speed	1.5 Sec max

Figure 4-8. *Table of timing specifications for signals*

Beside the tabulated timing schedule, a timing diagram is also utilized to visualize the timing constraints. Figure 4-9 is the example that Hatley and Pirbhai [1] have utilized. A timing diagram is a very useful tool to represent various timing characteristics side by side to organize and manage the control signals in addition of forming control patterns and themes.

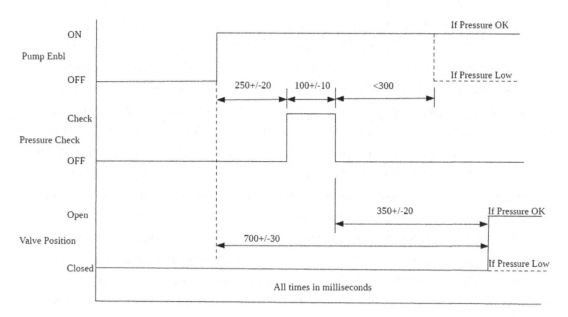

Figure 4-9. *Timing diagram for various signals*

A Note on Requirements Model

Although the HP method is a powerful tool to specify the product requirements, there are inherently a few somewhat major issues with it. Since this method was introduced at the time when CPM and CPD were at the height of their popularity, developing requirements through this method has a project-based outlook toward product development; and it is systematic, structured, and deterministic. However, developing PSPECs and CSPECs at the beginning of the development would be ideal if all the changes during the discovery phase are identified and all the project objectives at the beginning of the development phase are clear and well-defined. However, we know this will never happen. In the real world these and many other aspects of the project are subject to change. Additionally, the P and CSPEC documents do not cover the majority of product development activities of which many have tremendous impact on product and development. To name a few, they are manufacturing, prototyping, optimization, engineering and manufacturing testing, and so forth.

So why am I discussing the HP method here? It's because despite the fact that the world is not a perfect place and having a detailed and deterministic plan for a project that can be easily breached by changes is impractical, we must have short-term plans with clear objectives. I am looking for a middle ground in between complete chaos and absolute organization. In our approach, the short-term objectives based on empirical data are good enough to develop PSPEC and CSPEC documents for each layer of product. In other words, we won't have one single PSPEC and CSPEC document that defines the entire project. Each layer of PBS has PSPEC and CSPEC documents that are live documents. As we progress deeper into the lower layers of the product the upper layers become more deterministic. This is how we build up confidence in our development. We are still following a deterministic and structured framework, but at the same time we have created a good degree of freedom to accept unforeseen changes. As we explained earlier, the cone of uncertainty about the project/product scopes and features narrows down as the project/product development sprints toward the release date.

The moral of the story here is to develop a general description for each layer of PBS and be open to visit it again for revisions and expansions. This in Scrum is called "Inspect and Adapt," similar to the iterative "Design and Review" process in the V-Model; however in Scrum this process is confined within each Sprint but we expect to perform these activities throughout the project in order to redefine the scopes and features even for the past activities. Why for the past activities, you might ask? Because as it has been observed for the Scrum-based development, fine-tuning the previous features leads us to get a better picture of the future features and activities resulting in slimming down the future tasks. By now, it should be clear that by doing this we change the weight of the future tasks by balancing them out with respect to what has been completed.

Hatley and Pirbhai [1] talk about Process Model extensively. They covered a number of practices including methods on archiving and numbering the records. Their method is more fit for the time that archiving paper copies was required as one of the few means of communications and record retention. However, in the age of cloud storage and computing, piling up papers would be a costly and time-consuming practice. We can discuss the basics of data processing here and it would be up to you to decide how to carry out the process. Normally a real-time system faces two types of data and various data handling methods. The data can be categorized to two groups, external and internal. The external data is what is being fed to the system from outside via Input and Output Processing units and also a User Interface unit. The internal data is what the Main Control and Monitoring unit generates as a result of receiving external data. In the digital world, unless a massive amount of EMI exists or system design is flawed, the internal data behave predictably; therefore there is no need to frequently check the integrity of the internal data.

However since the external data comes from an analog world, it is prone to all sorts of noise and perturbations. It is fair to say that typically in a real-time system, a large portion of firmware and hardware is utilized to safeguard the integrity of external data. This includes all the software routines, hardware protection components, nonvolatile off-chip memories, and so forth. Manufacturing processes that employ various methods such as checking data ranges, user inputs and data-type limits, hardware component characterization, calibration, self-test, auto-tuning, safety-monitoring, and so forth are also considered as part of external data safeguarding methods. The majority of these are designed because of the human factors. For example, many electric motors encounter violent vibration at certain frequencies where the inputted frequency matches the fundamental or high-order natural frequency of the motor. A well-informed user will avoid these frequencies, however, to protect the motors from users' mistakes that the motor drive manufactures including predefined frequency bands called skip bands. If a misinformed user accidentally sets the frequency in these skip bands, the set frequency would jump up or down, not allowing the user to operate in these bands. Creating these skip bands are a complex task with complex algorithms since you have several bands that can overlap each other. Algorithms like these do not directly contribute to the motor's main function but they are there to protect the motor. These additional tasks, components, and algorithms are often considered as overhead to the core functionality of the system, but unfortunately necessary evil for various reasons.

In reference to documenting control and data flow of your system, it's worth to mention that Hatley and Pirbhai [1] went into details on how to carry out the requirements model for a real-time system with respect to CSPEC and PSPEC, which are Control and Process Specifications respectively. They illustrated a very comprehensive model that would satisfy the most difficult clients, such as military and medical specifications in terms of document traceability. However since the time their concept is introduced the computers have greatly changed the landscape of modern communications, including documentation processes. As we highlighted before, the modeling tools have blurred the line between documentation and product development, lending a helping hand to Agile methodologies. However, modeling, simulations, rapid prototyping and UML tools in no way have brain of their own therefore, having a well-thought architectural perspective of the entire system is absolutely necessary. In addition, documentation and traceability is still one of the major requirements for various industries including but not limited for military and medical applications.

Structured Scrum

So far we have discussed two major outlooks in life of modern product development and project management. One is project-based and deterministic in nature, which in a classical fashion uses CPM as a tool for project management and the Requirements Model to be used in the planning phase of real-time system projects and follows a CPD developmental model. The other one is process based and empirical in nature and called Agile methodology, which follows no specific structure. The structured Scrum is the middle ground, combining the goods of both worlds by empowering the product architects to also manage the development process since. Let's remember that we learned from the requirements model that process is in the heart of product architecture. The structured Scrum is organized enough to create effective communication channels and it's agile enough to reduce unnecessary organizational constraints.

Although Scrum is the most successful and pragmatic method in software development, its main shortcoming is to follow its co-location principal where most of today's engineering team is composed of members who are spread across the globe. To overcome the lack of co-location, the use of requirements model becomes more important than ever. A requirement model ensures that we establish a clear communication channel to the parties involved with developing the product. This by itself would have a tremendous impact on the quality of the work, cost of development, and the product time to market. However a requirement model as we know, is largely massive and definitely not Agile.

Now the question is, if we want to have an Agile and robust product development process, what should it look like? To achieve a robust and Agile process we need more than combining the classical and Agile methodologies. We should think out-of-the-box and look into the origin of these methods and the reason behind why they were invented. In previous chapters we tried to cover the most iconic tools in project management and product development methods and now we know enough about them that we can understand the principals of structured Scrum.

Simplified V-Model

You might have noticed in our earlier discussion about the V-Model that the requirements, design. and implementation phases in this model and CPD are very similar. Also often in the real world the same team of developers works on these phases. If we were to use any of Modeling Languages or MBD tools, the requirement, design, and implementation phases can be bundled up to one super phase. This is because these tools enable you to use the modeling environment for all three phases. If we combine these three phases of the V-Model, the resultant phase will be longer in duration than each individual phase but shorter than cumulative phases. However the deployment phase would be much shorter than its respective phase in the traditional model.

Figure 4-10 illustrate the use of Scrum utilizing Model-based development tools. The first release, Release A, would be comprised of only high-level models outlining the overall architectural modules of the system but also at the same time becoming a working prototype with limited features and functionalities. This release might be limited in features and functions but it is covers the entire product. Later we will learn how the MIL, SIL, and HIL methods can help to create a working prototype at this level.

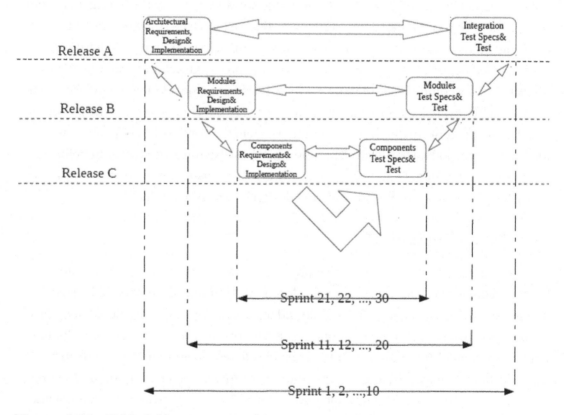

Figure 4-10. *V-Model in a structured Scrum environment*

Once the high-level system is designed we can move to the lower level and expand the functionalities and add more features to the product. The release B of our product would be significantly functional but not complete.

On the component level, which we'd like to call it Release C of the product, the modules of the higher level would be detailed out with components. This release would present our product, wholesome in features and complete in functionalities.

One should take caution as this development model is still project based and deterministic in nature, hence very rigid against accepting unforeseen changes in development, the changes which are the consequence of knowledge gained about our product's capabilities and limitations. On the other hand, we know a real-time system development is not just the software development but also the hardware design, implementation, and testing along with additional major developmental activities such as manufacturing.

But keep in mind that it is the software that always creates a bottleneck in the project, not hardware. If we could give a head start to the software activities by letting them start sooner, then we could remove this bottleneck. But we know the software must run on a hardware platform and often needs to be tested under a load or on a plant hardware. As we discussed before at the prototyping section, the project developers can utilize MIL, SIL, HIL, or any combination of them until the hardware is developed. Therefore as parts of product hardware become available to the software development team the prototype could gradually remove the development dependencies from in-the-loop parts and rely more on the actual hardware. This approach has also numerous other benefits for hardware development by reducing the hardware bugs, faster hardware development, and achieving a more optimized hardware design in size and function.

Continuous Integration

Continuous Integration (CI) is a popular process in software development but it can also be carried out for the real-time system development. Assuming the embedded system development is heavy on the software side and lighter on the hardware side, by defining a suitable system architectural model, one can still carry out an effective CI process for the real-time systems. The continuous integration in software environment is mainly to build the code that is being checked in to a common repository. It can be as simple as building the code or as complex as building and testing the code at the same time. In an embedded environment we can apply the same concept to hardware and software simultaneously. But keep in mind that the frequency of software changes significantly outnumbers the hardware build versions. While a software build number can increment several times a day, a hardware build number might increment once per few months. But this won't change our CI process. Any changes on the software or hardware side can trigger a CI process.

It is up to the architect to coordinate between hardware and software development, which the continuous integration process would follow accordingly. The CIs can be categorized to major and minor or in a Scrum environment to CIs dedicated to epics and stories respectively. The epic CIs occur when a new version of hardware introduced to the development and story CIs assigned to software development. This will elevate our understanding of the CI concept from a software-only process to a product development process.

Progressive Product Test

Based on the HP method, process development is part of the requirements model and a requirements model builds the product architecture. In every facet of product development whether in hardware or software, the end of development is considered a major milestone and it is preceded by passing a set of acceptance criteria in the form of validation tests. By now we should all agree that before achieving any milestone in our developmental process, we should plan and perform testing. In Scrum, a test should validate the state of potentially shippable product. This test looks a lot like the End of Line testing in the manufacturing environment. CPD also has the same type of testing right before the product launch when the engineering and manufacturing checked samples are being distributed among various engineering groups to be validated. In a software development according to the V-Model, integration, module and component testing are considered to be milestone tests. Some companies have started introducing smoke tests in their Agile processes that do the same thing as milestone tests with a difference that it can be carried out much more frequently than other comparable tests in other development environment.

Let's step back for a moment and look at the concept of test as a whole and think what the real purpose is of testing during development? In classical methods whether it was V-Model or CPD, in hardware or software departments, the test is always a sign of achieving a new milestone at the end of each phase. In Scrum also, testing is to verify if the story has met the acceptance criteria. Once all stories in a sprint are reached, the same level of success than the product is potentially ready to be shipped. All these tests in different developmental environments are there to test the product. After the product is passed the research phase, all the tests perfumed on the product during development are to verify and validate, not to discover. In development, we aren't doing scientific testing to discover new things; we do all these to see if we have achieved the level of confidence in our product, which can allow us to release it into the hands of customers.

Since all development teams perform milestone testing at various release stages, we can always find useless redundant test routines performed concurrently on the same product. This is because the lower-level tests often are subset of higher-level product testing. The lack of interdepartmental communications, proper product documentation, and the hovering hammer of project managers rushing the developers through the development makes it very easy to create unnecessary test activities. Right now, somewhere in the world, a team of manufacturing engineers are struggling to come up with a functional test procedure for which the research team has had to face and then overcame the same challenge months earlier but failed to document and communicate their achievements with the teams downstream.

However there might be a way to reduce the unnecessary redundancies and to minimize this massive amount of waste in development. In the next example we borrow the "Smoke Test" concept from the software development and merge it with the Scrum's shippable product concept; then we create a testing stage – a recurring milestone test before each product release. Let's call this test the "product test," whether it tests only a blinking LED or is intended to test a fantastic light show for a legendary Rock-n'-Roll band.

Flat V-Model

A flat V-Model is a modified V-Model to be followed during a Sprint in Scrum. Since Scrum has its own iterative process of inspect and adapt, also, considering the duration of a Sprint is much shorter than the product's life cycle in a V-Model, we no longer need the feedback process of design and review during a Sprint. All the design feedback will be added as an item to the backlog. Also, since the concept and release phases are very short and happen very frequent in every Sprint we can simplify the V-Model as it is shown in Figure 4-11.

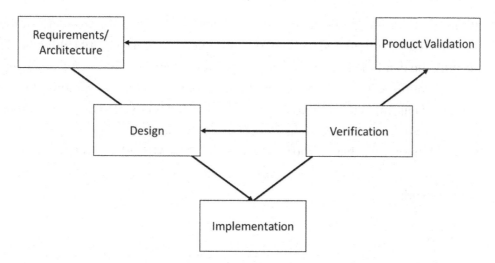

Figure 4-11. *Revised V-Model with Omitted Concept and Release Phases*

The next simplification happens as a direct benefit of utilizing Scrum and Continuous Integration concept. As we discussed it before, the testing activities on the system, module, and component levels happen at the same time. So we can further simplify the V-Model as in Figure 4-12.

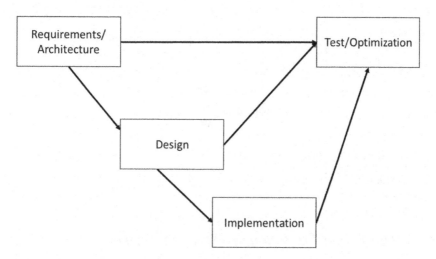

Figure 4-12. *V-Model, Further Modified for Scrum*

Furthermore, let's imagine you have only two weeks to finish your product. For the given time, testing requirements/architecture, modules, and components individually while meeting the deadline in two weeks would be almost impossible. If you are using an automated continue integration concept then as soon as a change happens, the test will be triggered automatically. Therefore, all your developers need to do is to test their assigned components, making sure they won't break the build. They develop their test cases then add them to the list for the product testing. The MIL, SIL, and HIL now will be doing the rest of the testing activities. Figure 4-13 shows the concept of a flat V-Model in a Scrum framework.

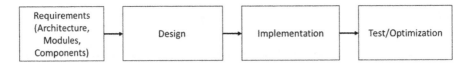

Figure 4-13. *Scrum-based flat V-Model*

Figure 4-14 shows the case when the flat V-Model is utilized during many Sprint iterations.

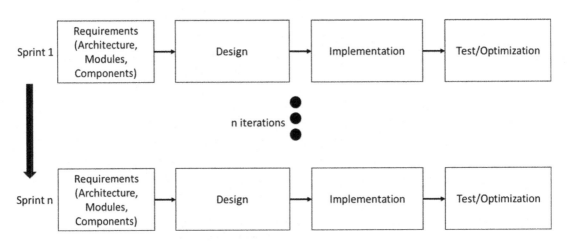

Figure 4-14. *Flat V-Model in Action in a Scrum framework*

An Example of a New Product Development

Let's assume we are required to develop a minimum number of modules to perform the absolute minimum core functionality of a real-time system. We are also required to have a single algorithm in the core processing unit in order to satisfy the absolute minimum marketing/customer requirements for a function that would satisfy the acceptance criteria so the product can be pronounced a "potentially shippable product." Now let's see if we can merge the CPD into the V-Model so our software development would be more stakeholder friendly.

We do this because there are many similarities between these two, so merging should be easy. But the main purpose behind all these is that by migrating CPD to V-Model we make the software the main driving force in embedded system development; and also as you can see later it is easier to modify the V-Model in order to make it Agile friendly. Making a CPD process Agile friendly would be much harder because CPD is a framework for the entire project, mostly used by the stakeholders as a decision-making tool. V-Model, on the other hand, is a product life-cycle road map, designed specifically for software development. However V-Model can be used for the hardware development if it's merged with CPD.

As we discussed, the minimum number of modules that any real-time system needs to incorporate in order to become a true "potentially shippable product" needs to have four main modules: the user interface, system inputs, system outputs, and the main processing unit. This is also the base of our system architecture.

In Chapter 3 we discussed that the system architecture comprises hardware and software architectures. Earlier we saw that the idea for creating a flat V-Model was to squeeze the entire CPD/V-Model phases into any Sprint of our new Structured Scrum process. As you can see in Figure 4-15, for each development effort at the architectural level there will be a minimum of 4 tasks on the modular level and 16 tasks on the design level. This is because for each architectural modules of 4 essentials (user interface, system inputs and outputs, and main processing unit), there will be four design-level tasks (Module Requirement Development, Module design, Module Implementation, and Module Testing) for each module and if there is only one component per module, then there will be also four component level tasks (Component Requirement Development, Component Design, Component Implementation, and Component Testing).

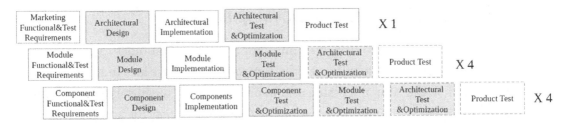

Figure 4-15. *A flat V-Model visualization in a Scrum environment for each module comprising only one component*

But doing all these nine activities for each main module, we still would not be able to encompass the notion of "a potentially shippable product." We need to perform 4 module optimizations and tests, 1 architectural optimization and test, and 1 product test. Each hardware and software development process needs the same minimum number of tasks. Technically in a V-Model, the tests performed for the architectural/requirement level are same as product test but this is for a pure software product. You can apply the same principles to the hardware development and then merge the hardware and software product test in a single test.

Since hardware, software, and manufacturing development might not progress as the same pace, or there might be some expected lapses due to readiness, having to design architectural structures for each will allow some flexibilities in order to synchronize all the project activities. Scrum tries to address this synchronization issue through introducing the T-shape skill set concept in sprint activities. This issue was initially identified by CPM and their remedy was to delay, break up, and overlap tasks in order to level resource utilizations, ideally utilizing all the project resources at a constant rate of 100% for every working day.

However, there is a problem with both methods. In Scrum, the T-shape skill set concept works for similar stories under one engineering discipline, which is mostly software engineering; but in reality, you don't see every day a software specialist to work on the hardware. In CPM, introducing delays in a project that is deadline driven seems to be defeating the purpose of project management. The solution to the resource utilization and also tasks synchronization problem is to introduce architectural structure for each of these special project functions with their prospective engineering disciplines involved. After we create the architecture layer and their subsequent modules and components, then we can identify task components that can share the common resources across the entire project.

The identification of task and their necessary resources shouldn't happen at the end of the project planning like how CPM treats this problem. This activity can be activated as soon as the first version of our shippable product of the project is introduced. In the following picture, we see three major life cycles for the product of each major engineering discipline, which are lending their hand to create the final product. Each life cycle has its own product with a flat V-Model life cycle.

As we explained before, from a flat V-Model we have an architectural layer. If our potentially shippable product is ready at the end of this phase then all three V-Models can share one common test phase that is the product test; if not then we proceed with each V-Model until all three converge to this first shippable product. The natural choice would be to form the shippable product as early as possible preferably at the concept phase. If it's not then each life cycle has its own product test phase: for example, we would have three separate products test at the end of each phase of manufacturing, hardware, and software development. In addition, as the project pans out, the details of the product emerge more clearly, which can help to identify what task components can be shared among our resources. The goal is to converge all the parallel development activities at one point. Please see Figure 4-16.

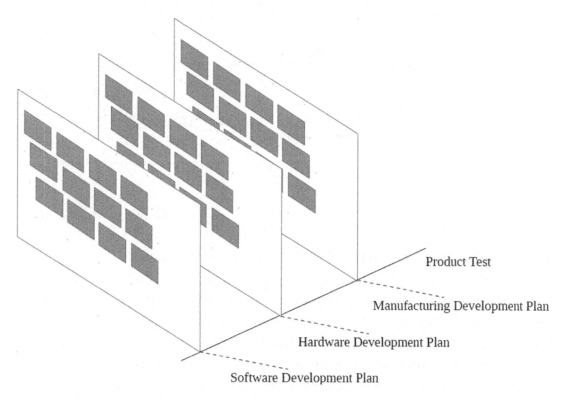

Figure 4-16. *Flat V-Model for various engineering functions during product development*

PBS Development

As we previously discussed, the building blocks of any architecture are components. Components also make modules, which is another way to take functionally similar components under one module. In the real-time systems there are two major functionalities: control-based functionalities and data-based functionalities. An efficient architecture will try to have one layer for all controls and a different one for data layers. Depending on the size and complexity of design there might be a need to create interface to connect one data module to another or one data module to a control module. These interfaces either reside on their own layers or take part in the existing data or control layers. This all completely depends on where your system architecture will take you. All control and data modules and components carry information via data and control buses. Figure 4-17 shows the Data Buses are comprised of several Data Signals. In a programming environment these buses will be translated to the data structures.

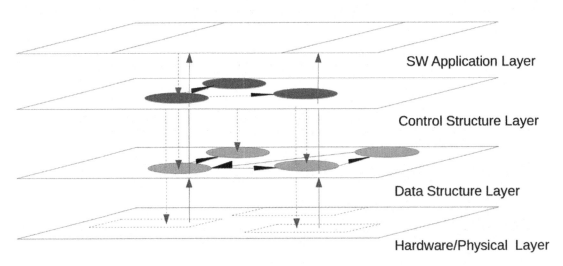

Figure 4-17. *How DFD and CFD interact in a Layers environment*

We should perform the same process to the control layer and try to keep the data separate from the control elements including the buses and signals. This will greatly reduce the programming bugs and will expose the design and implementation flaws, allowing clear and transparent interfaces to form. Another advantage of separating the control and data signals is to break down complex elements of designs into much simpler components. So you must always separate the data from control.

Each level of product design can be consistent with a minimum of four layers: Application Software layer, Control and Data Firmware layers, and hardware physical layer. For example, for turning an LED on an electronics board, we might need to touch all four layers, from GUI on the host PC to a central control unit in the firmware in order to carry out a simple task. Figure 4-15 depicts a template of what you would normally expect to see in a PBS.

As an example, a software application layer has more overall control over the whole product functionality but the control is in terms of user commands. The software control layer on the other hand has a better grip on product function. So from a software perspective, the software application layer defines the architecture layer of our software. Since the architecture is the result of requirements, consequently, customer stipulation directly translates to application software. The application software then will drive the lower control and data layers, even the hardware physical layer. This is the true meaning of requirements traceability. The spirit on the customer's requirements then will also drive manufacturing processes by defining the product.

The question here would be how these product functionality layers fit into our flat V-Model? The software application layer, as we expressed, clearly falls into the software architecture layer, which will serve the marketing requirements closely. This layer might be also supported by a hardware architecture layer in terms of displays and the means of system inputs and outputs. What comes after are the module and components either with software or hardware platforms. Having a flat V-Model for each one of these developments can help to align the hardware and software components to converge to a certain point at one time in the near future.

The underlying ideal concept is that we try to advance all the layers involved at the same pace with a uniform complexity. This is another reason we need to form our first potentially shippable product as early in development as possible, which means it requires that we should focus our activities to develop our product initially in its most basic form. We will explain this later in greater detail. At this point we explore the design approaches for each level whether it's at architecture, module, submodule, or component levels.

Additionally, when you are developing the PBS, do not apply any constraints whether they are physical, logical or resource-based on your product design. The nature of constraints has nothing to do with how a module should function. If you do not have enough staff for designing a control algorithm it shouldn't mean to have some product features and functions underdeveloped. Let the Agile framework worry about the resource planning and scope modification.

A Different Approach in Design

We discussed the decompositions rules a little earlier. We now know that the software application layer is an architectural layer; therefore it follows the architectural template that we described earlier. The software application layer might have a hardware layer that directly supports it, such as LCD displays, keyboards, sensors, and so forth; however the interaction between this layer and hardware might not be as direct as it seems. Depending on the complexity of the application, our system is required to carry out, we might need some intermediary layers to connect the dots in between our user interface and the hardware. We might also need two or more sets of architectural layers for our application: one on the hardware side and the other on the software platform.

The picture in Figure 4-18 only depicts the data architecture from the data layer. The breaking-down rule is exactly as you are developing a WBS for a Gantt Chart or composing a Backlog for your next sprint. As you saw, we call this a product breakdown structure (PBS). Obviously when there is a data PBS there must be also a control PBS. The control PBS is not shown here. Defining and organizing the relationship between a control and data PBS are going to be explored later in detail. Again when you are developing your requirements model you are also creating your PBS.

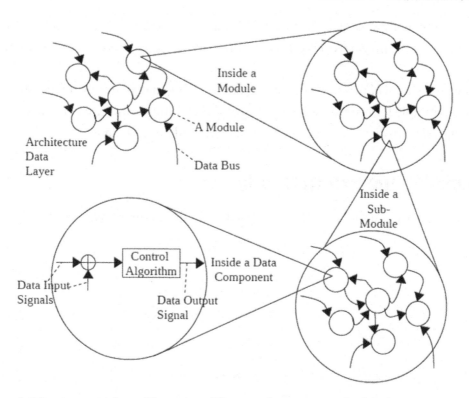

Figure 4-18. *A reminder of functional hierarchy in an embedded system*

Please note that in order to minimize the number of algebraic operations at the higher layers, do the least or no operations you have to and wait until you are at the component level of your product. Be careful when you are developing your requirements model and PBS, not to share modules/ components with other modules/components. It is ok to have identical submodules/components and let the architecture and tools decide to handle this situation. This is because at this stage of function definition, your goal is to identify functionalities involved with constructing modules. As you can see later there will come a phase called design optimization that will allow us do just that.

As we stated before, we should never overdesign. Your focus should be to develop very simple modules as there will be many opportunities later to complicate things. Simple design has another significant advantage: it will set the stakeholders' expectations at a manageable level. The combination of all these simple components will make your system a mighty complex and capable system at the end. Depending on the size of our team, we can have people work on developing control and data paths independently because the design is now divided into independent layers. Later you can marry these layers for final product deliverables at each product release. Using finite state machine methodologies are always helpful for the systems with critical control objectives because they have a modular nature and are much more in lined with the PBS approach.

Since the size of efforts and code involved regarding data handling in any real-time system is multiple fold compared to control and algorithm efforts and code, in the next two paragraphs we discuss how to handle external and internal data.

Processing the External Data

Consider the system template in Figure 4-19 that we discussed earlier:

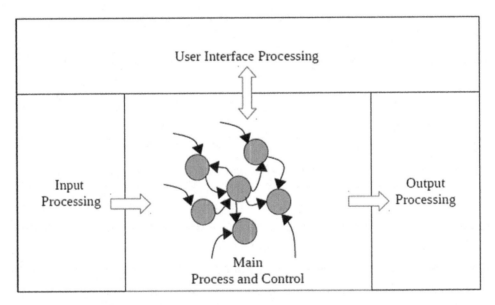

Figure 4-19. *A reminder of functional modules in the grand view of system architecture*

Any data that passes through the boundaries of the central unit, which in here is called Main Process and Control, is considered external data. This includes the user data such as set points, limits, ranges, and scaling factors and also the values that are read and written via the external component such as sensors, switches, and actuators, whether they are of a continuous or discrete nature.

A common recurring theme in external data processing with respect to data handling is that the data integrity, due to noise and user errors, needs to be checked frequently. To save some crucial code space and microprocessor time we can perform much of the external data handling locally at the user interface or sensor level (smart sensors). From the architectural perspective these functions still will be on a data layer but will be marked to be executed locally. Additionally, some of this processing can be performed in the hardware such as RLC filters but with an additional cost. From the requirements model and PBS points of view, these are design constraints that need to be addressed at a later time by the corresponding functional teams.

Processing the Internal Data

The internal data is assumed to be uncorrupted unless your algorithm software, hardware design with respect to PCB layout, EMI shielding, and so forth are flawed. For this very reason the processes that you put in place at the user interfaces to validate the data integrity, filtering the noise, or preventing the user errors need not be employed for the internal data processing. However you might need to employ some handshaking mechanism to validate the data such as using checksum algorithms and so on to validate the internal data occasionally.

In addition, we should be mindful of brief, descriptive, intuitive, and consistent naming conventions for the data flows. The data flow/buses must be defined in a homogeneous format in a place called the data dictionary. The data dictionary would also include the list of abbreviations used throughout the design documents. To get a better idea, consider an industrial or civil engineering drawing. The document must be intuitive to follow and must be all inclusive of terms, special notes, symbols, and instructions so that the user can follow and build the system. It is not our goal to create documents. Our duty is to create a cost-effective product in an efficient way. The documentation is only a vehicle taking us to these objectives.

Operating Systems, a Proper Mean of Data Handling

Unfortunately, the majority of software and firmware engineers in the real-time system development environment are not aware of the science behind software engineering. In the majority of companies the firmware engineers come from a hardware background and to them OS's are there only to create software overhead. However in real life and due to the ever-increasing complexity of the modern applications, it is OK to pay for some extra memory to have a more deterministic and secure data handling process in our processors.

In addition, many of the modern real-time operating systems provide us with debugging tools that are proven to be vital in shortening the troubleshooting time and securing a quicker time to market while guaranteeing the data integrity with high confidence. On the other hand, the use of operating systems goes hand in hand with the use of databases, which are a means to create uniform data interfacing systems.

Databases in Real-Time Systems

Another foreign concept to most firmware engineers who develop real-time systems is how to develop and utilize various types of databases in the embedded system development. Similar to operating systems, the databases are also used to organize the data and feed the computational engines with a timely stream of data. This ensures the data integrity for a small cost of additional memory and processor utilizations. One of the most popular method of databases is the producer-consumer scheme. This pattern is most useful where some of the system functions run at different speeds and there are many producer and consumers contributing to the same sets of data. A producer would queue the data for a consumer to grab at its earliest possible time.

Bringing It All Together

The idea here, as we discussed before, is to follow a CPD/V-Model life cycle in an Agile and structured Scrum format. Why a structured Scrum format and not a popular Scrum format? It's because Scrum is not designed to address hardware aspects of the real-time systems and it also does not reflect the reality of today's global engineering efforts. Also, why do we want our development to be in an Agile framework? This is because the CPD and CPM were introduced for a different sets of problems. Software is increasingly becoming the dominant part of the real-time system development and the quality of it has become the major concern of other engineering disciplines.

Figure 4-20 illustrates the idea of layers architecture, which will be extensively explained in the later chapters. Considering the essential development layers involved in producing a real-time system product consists of two major layers, data and control; additional auxiliary layers can be added under the coverage of system architecture, manufacturing, and hardware layers. A CPD or a Modified V-Model would touch each layer through a vertical slice at each iteration of the product development especially at the product release milestones. While from the outside world the progress of the product looks familiar as a CPD progression, at each slice all layers of the product will be touched by the CPD's phases.

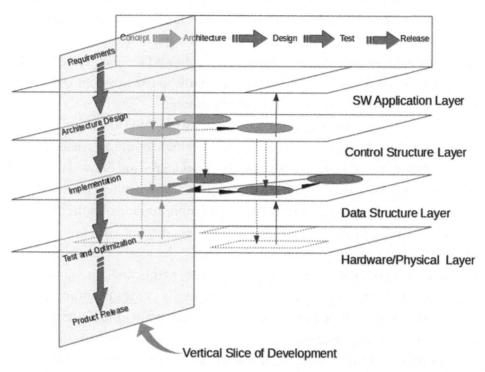

Figure 4-20. *Bringing functions and forms together by integrating Layers model in the product development model*

As the product progresses through the horizontal axis there will be more emphasis on that phase on the vertical axis. For example at the concept phase on the horizontal axis, the manufacturing engineering activities focus more on the prototyping and proof of concept tasks. Since at this stage the activities would be around prototyping, a minimum amount of optimizations and implementation would take effect and the majority of the efforts would be on POC. This trend will continue and each time the bulk of developmental activities would focus on the phases on the horizontal axis.

Utilizing MBD Tools for PBS

As Hatley and Pirbhai explained in their book, creating the process specification (PSPEC) and control specifications (CPSEC) are to document what the objective of each layer of PBS is. In an MBD environment there is no need for this because the design diagrams along the usage of proper naming conventions, legends, and design hierarchy will be self-explanatory. In addition, the MBD tools will greatly help in developing the necessary documentation embedded in the modeling environment.

If there is one strong reason to justify the added cost of MBD tools for the project stakeholders and the dinosaurs in the finance, it is to create a strong case for the amount of energy, time, and effort these tools save at the PBS and onward phases. As we discussed earlier there will be many design revisions and implementation iterations. MBD tools can make the process of reshuffling, recombining, and repartitioning the modules much more manageable and less tedious than they normally are.

In addition, having reliable design tools will free up the team's brain power at the decomposition stage so they can focus on functionality of the modules rather than worrying prematurely on how to cope with the complexity of the oncoming modules and components. This is well aligned with the natural human brain function as the brain is more efficient in improving than creating. Once all the modules at one level are created, revising them would advance much faster and smoother. Therefore, the MBD tools will become increasingly useful at the design stage.

The additional and much appreciated feature of these tools is their ability to simulate the results. Working on a computer is faster and less expensive than hardware prototyping. Simulation also will establish design benchmarks that will greatly help the hardware and firmware troubleshooting at the implementation and optimization stages and later on in establishing pass and fail criteria at the manufacturing stage.

Summary

Through reading this chapter, we learned to organize a project around a product, not tasks. We should let the product dictate what needs to be done, not what we think needs to be done. The product already exists through marketing requirements and customers' demands, so the developers are there to materialize it.

The first step in any product development methodology is developing the first prototype. We like to call it the first potentially shippable product. It doesn't matter what we call it, but a first prototype is one that includes the main functionality of the product envisioned in the MRD. It will look ugly, bulky, and primitive but it proves the original concept. This would be the keystone of our project.

The first release of our potentially shippable product will be heavily reflective of product architecture in hardware and software. The product test will be performed before each release, and it will slice through all the product layers starting from, hardware, to control, data, and finally software application layers. The nature of test will be regressive and it will grow with the product.

Finally, we'd like to see that the product development follows an Agile methodology, which is based on the HP requirements model and follows a modified V-Model in a two-dimensional CPD framework. We call this new Agile method a structured Scrum. The first dimension of the CPD runs in every sprint to make sure communication channels are clear and the second CPD runs in the life line of the project to interface with the stakeholders. As the product progresses across its life line from one phase to another CPD to another, the emphasis on that CPD phase will get stronger. Agile creates organization from chaos. Just gather the expertise needed and then let the teams self-organize. It's all common sense.

Bibliography

[1] Harley, Derek J., and Imtiaz A. Pirbhai, *Strategies for Real-Time System Specifications.* New York: Dorset House Publishing Co. Inc., 1988, p. 274.

CHAPTER 5

Problem Statement

The scope of this chapter is to build a requirements model based on a product in its classical form. What we discuss here covers only the basics. We don't go into much details because this particular paper-based management system was most practical before personal computers introduced us to the world of a paperless information management system. In the chapter after this, the same example will be presented but with a difference, that is, we will construct the entire project in a structured Scrum framework utilizing MBD. The following example from the Hatley and Pirbhai [1].

The customer requirements developed here is a new embedded real-time product for a smart automobile management system:

- Cruise Control: The driver can choose to activate the system in order to maintain a constant speed. The system should be designed in a manner that gives the driver total control to interrupt the system via brake and accelerator pedals or manual control.

- Average Speed Monitoring: The driver by pushing the start trip button will acquire the average speed of the vehicle for the entire trip.

- Fuel Consumption Monitoring: The driver at each refueling stage can add the amount of fuel and ask the system to calculate and display the fuel consumption over the forthcoming period.

Understanding the Problem

Let's settle for a marketing definition of the system and ignore the architectural mandate for having three distinct modules. What they really meant was that they wanted a system that specifically addresses three functionalities. The subject of architectural layout of our real-time system is entirely an engineering process that must be left alone to the engineers to decide how to design the system based on various factors including system

125

© Mohsen Mirtalebi 2017
M. Mirtalebi, *Embedded Systems Architecture for Agile Development*,
https://doi.org/10.1007/978-1-4842-3051-0_5

resources, computational power, hardware design, and many other factors. However, it won't hurt, until we learn more about the problem at hand, to settle with the marketing's vision. To understand how these three functionalities correlate and coexist we need to attack the problem from various angles of which one of them would be the function diagram shown in Figure 5-1.

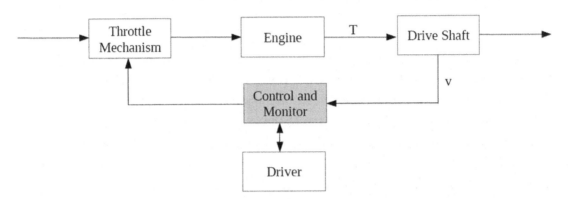

Figure 5-1. *A simple control diagram emphasizing the relationship between the user and the product*

The Control and Monitor unit is the system we are trying to develop. This is simply a graph that shows the relationship between our system and other major units in the vehicle. I marked the arrows of which I need to refer to in the text. The other arrows have less to no significance to our discussion. This diagram does not show any data and control flow. The driver sends and receives data and sends commands to the control and monitor unit. This unit controls the throttle mechanism through which the engine is controlled to produce appropriate torque (T). The drive shaft will convert the torque to velocity (v) and send the speed data to the control and monitor unit. Consequently, the data will be relayed to the driver for monitoring purposes.

Requirements Model

The requirements model at this stage will help us to decompose the functional requirements to much simpler and smaller parts. This process in its traditional form is not Agile friendly but can fit into a Scrum framework using a flat V-Model. However, for the sake of providing comparison, we do this example in its traditional format but in the next chapter we will utilize structured Scrum to develop the same example.

Data Context and Control Context Diagrams (DCD, CCD)

According to Hatley and Pirbhai [1], the first stage of the requirements model is to develop a DCD and CCD. As you might remember from the previous sections, these two diagrams show the relationship between the systems under development with the external parts. Therefore the Control and Monitor system needs to interact with brake, engine, drive shaft, driver, and throttle mechanism. The following graphs illustrate the data and control flows for the highest level of the requirements model. Figure 5-2 portrays the DCD.

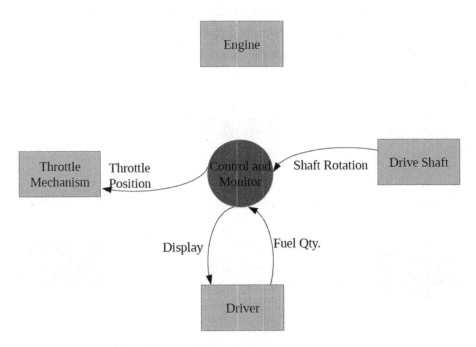

Figure 5-2. *DCD Graph of the product*

The engine unit does not need to send any data to our Control and Monitor or otherwise known as Electronics Control Module (ECM). This is because for our product, all we need from the engine is speed data, which can get from the drive shaft unit. You might remember from the MRD, the driver needs to enter into the ECM the amount of fuel s/he put in the car's tank. That's why the data flow is toward the ECM, not the other way around. The ECM then will provide the driver with a bunch of data with respect to this specific application. Finally the ECM will provide the throttle mechanism to let the cruise control maintain speed.

As it is illustrated in Figure 5-3, the CCD mirrors the same components as DCD but for the purpose of showing the control flow at system level. This figure is especially interesting as you can distinguish between control and monitor signals applicability. The ECM receives the engine status from the engine unit and this would fulfill the purpose of monitoring for the ECM. On the other hand, the ECM receives control signals, here a command signal from driver. As you noticed, there is no command or monitoring signals from and to the drive shaft and throttle mechanism. The relationship was established through the data flow in Figure 5-2. In simple words, what connects the ECM to these units is the data. You might think there must be more signals connecting all these modules; however for this simple application and for the purpose of keeping the concept simple we should avoid overcomplicating the design at this stage. Later on when we learn more about our product and application, we can come back and revise these diagrams.

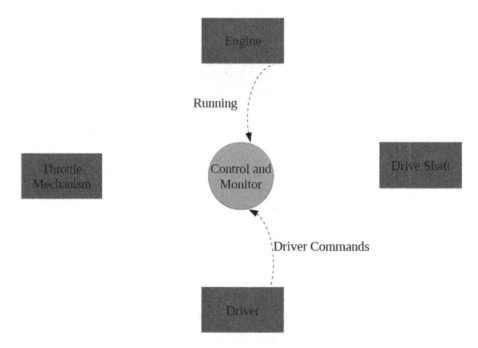

Figure 5-3. *CCD Graph of the product function*

Data Flow and Control Flow Diagrams (DFD, CFD)

At this level the functionality of the Control and Monitor unit would be defined in a very abstract fashion. Let's start with DFD. The functions within the large dotted circles are the ones considered as the Control and Monitor unit and therefore it outlines our system that we intend to develop.

The DFD 0 and CFD 0 are the highest level of modules that express the system functions in its initial stage. Then DFD and CFD graphs would be gradually decomposed to smaller and more detailed contents. After all, the PSPEC and CSPEC would be developed according to these contents.

Since this is a simple example, the Measure Motion and Measure Mile modules won't be decomposed to the smaller components. Therefore, we will directly address their functionalities in their respective PSEPCs. On the other hand the Control Throttle and Monitor Status modules are more complex; hence we will go one layer deeper in DFD and CFD so we could address their complexities with a more detailed explanation for their function definitions.

Figure 5-4 shows both DFD and CFD for our first module, control and monitor. This module comprises of four submodules. If you can be patient at the PSPEC and CSPEC levels we will discuss the functionalities and flows of each submodule in detail. The rule of thumb is that, if there is a module with data and control flows attached to them, they need to be decomposed to smaller pieces until they cannot be broken down further. This is where we need the PSPECs and CSPECs to define the functions of these components via formulas or pseudo-codes.

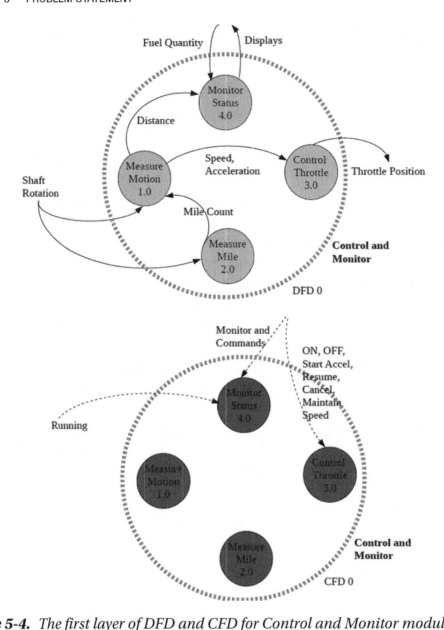

Figure 5-4. *The first layer of DFD and CFD for Control and Monitor module*

After finishing the first and second layers of the requirements model, we can proceed to the next level. The title of this level of DFDs and CFDs is accompanied with a number that denotes the corresponding number on the prior level. For example, control throttle is denoted with number 3.0. The title of the next level DFD and CFD is accompanied with the number 3.0. Since the Measure Motion and Measure Mile modules are simple modules, there is no need for further DFD and CFD development. Therefore, the next requirement level of these modules will end in PSPECS and/or CSPECS. Figure 5-5 is the DFD for our next complex module, Control Throttle.

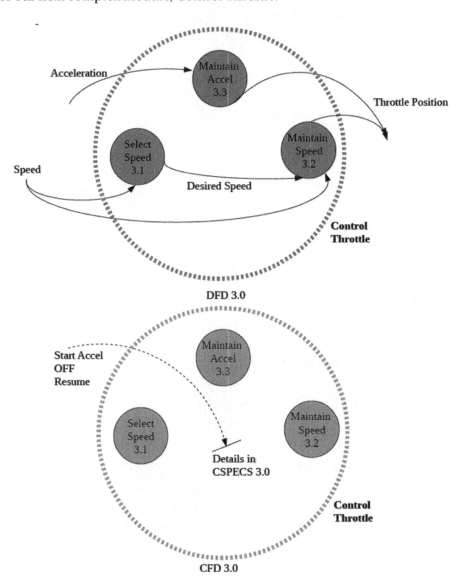

Figure 5-5. *The second layer of overall product function, DFD, and CFD of Control Throttle submodule*

From level 1, the only remaining module is Monitor Status to be broken down to more details. This module as you can see later is more complex and requires further decompositions. Figure 5-6 shows the data structure for our Monitor Status module, and Figure 5-7 shows the corresponding control structure.

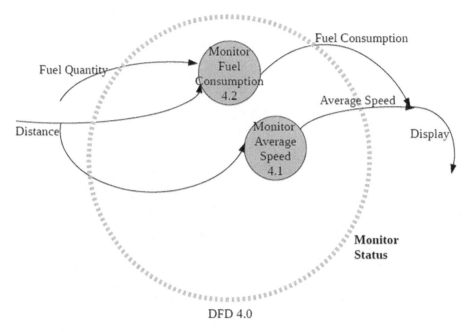

Figure 5-6. *The first layer of DFD for Monitor Status module*

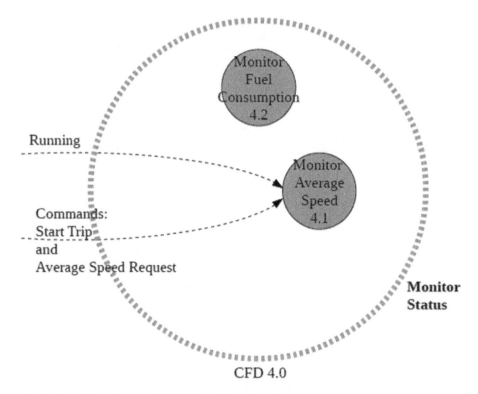

Figure 5-7. *The first layer of CFD for Monitor Status*

After finishing defining all the functionalities in the first layer of the requirements model, we can move on confidently to the next layer. Figure 5-8 shows the data and control structures for our first module in the second layer of our design, Monitor Average Speed submodule. Please note the dashed line ending in the middle of the diagram in CFD 4.1. These are HP's way of showing storing the parameter values in non-volatile memory locations to be passed on to other parameters. System flags and monitors are examples of utilizing this notation. The engine running status will be stored in a memory location that can be used by other modules at a later time.

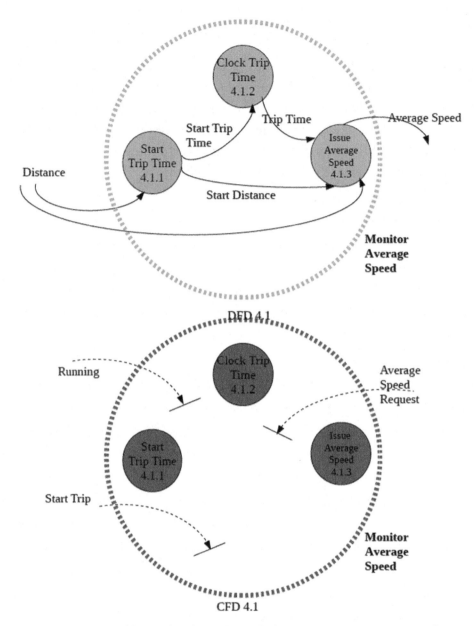

Figure 5-8. *The second layer for the submodule Monitor Average Speed*

PSPEC and CSPEC

It seems we have broken down the DFDs and CFDs to the extent that we are ready to draw the PSPECs and CSPECs to define the functionalities. The following is HP's pseudo-code to define these functions. As a kind reminder, please don't dwell too much on the accuracy of these formulas as they are defined in a digital domain and depending on your module dependencies and how your interrupt routines are structured, you might arrive in different versions of the same function definitions. Since we haven't defined our timing specifications yet, it's best that you bring only physical and mathematical formulas here rather than trying to write the program code at once. As I said this is just to show you can define your PSPECS and CSPECS in any fashion you see fits the best. You will see in the next chapter we will bypass these classical definitions all together and will utilize graphical methods in MBD.

PSPEC 1.0: Measure Motion

```
Distance_Count ++;
Distance = Distance_Count/Mile_Count;
Speed = Pulse_Rate/Mile_Count;
Accel = Rate_Change/Mile_Count;
```

The alternative description would be:

$$x = distance;$$
$$v = dx / dt = velocity;$$
$$a = dv / dt = acceleration;$$

PSPEC 2.0: Measure Mile

```
Shaft_Rotation_Pulse += ;
Calculate_Pulse_Count (Shaft_Rotation_Pulse);
If Lower_Limit<= Shaft_Rotation_Pulse <=Upper_Limit
        set Mile_Count = Shaft_Rotation_Pulse;
Otherwise
        set Mile_Count = Default_Mile_Count;
```

CSPEC 3.0: Control Throttle

ON, OFF, Start Accel, Resume, Cancel, Maintain Speed. Please see Figure 5-9 to see how these variables correlate in the Control Throttle state machine.

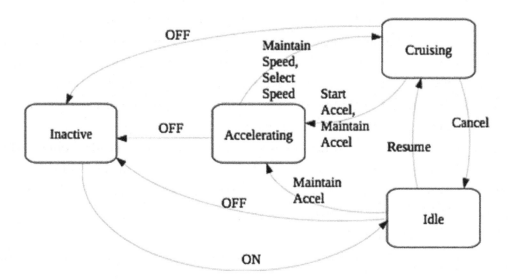

Figure 5-9. *A cruise control state machine to visualize the CSPEC of the Control Throttle module*

PSPEC 3.1: Select Speed

```
Issue Desired_Speed = Speed;
```

PSPEC 3.2: Maintain Speed

```
Throttle_Position  = 0 if Desired_Speed - Current_Speed > 2
                   = 2*(Desired_Speed - Current_Speed) if -2 <=Desired_
                   Speed - Current_Speed <= 2
                   = 8 if Desired_Speed - Current_Speed < -2
```

PSPEC 3.3: Maintain Accel

```
Throttle_Position  = 0 if Acceleration > 1.2
                   = 20*(1..2-Acceleration) if 0.8<= Acceleration <=1.2
                   = 8 if Acceleration < 0.8
```

CSPEC 4.1: Monitor Average Speed

```
Start Trip Time will activate process 4.1.1
Running will activate process 4.1.2
Average Speed Request will activate process 4.1.3
```

PSPEC 4.1.1: Start Trip Time

```
Issue Trip_Time = 0;
Issue Start_Distance = Distance;
```

PSPEC 4.1.2: Clock Trip Time

```
Accumulate seconds for every second the process is on;
```

PSPEC 4.1.3: Issue Average Speed

```
Issue Average_Speed = (Distance - Start_Distance)/Trip_Time;
```

PSPEC 4.2: Monitor Fuel Consumption

```
Issue Fuel_Consumption = (Distance - Start_Distance)/Fuel_Qty;
then set Refuel_Distance = Distance;
```

Please note the PSPEC and CSPEC are not design specifications nor are they there to replace them. In our example we utilized various formats from Pseudo-Codes, to C-codes, mathematical equations, and a state machine to represent the functionalities of the components. At this stage you should not bound yourself to a specific format to express functions. The goal is to describe a function in the clearest way, quickly.

Timing Specification

Obviously, HP's philosophy was hinged on project-based product development and as a result the requirements model is very deterministic in nature and in a stark contrast with more modern Agile methodologies, which are more fluid about team dynamics and product architecture. The timing specification is an example of rigidity of HP's method but in some applications it's a necessity. However with MBD tools, you can have come up with your own timing method that fits your application where you can simulate the system in non or real-time environments to find out whether your timing schemes meet the requirements.

The first step in developing your own timing spec is to create a Time response schedule for each transition action in your CEPCs. For example, in Figure 5-9. all the transition actions in our state machine can be specified in a table in Figure 5-10. This table shows the time responses as well as the dependencies between the functions. With this in mind now we can develop our own timing specification that is the collection of the timing responses of all CSPECs actions.

Input	Event	Output	Event	Response Time
ON	Turns on	Throttle Position	Goes to idle state	0.5 sec max
Resume	Turns on	Throttle Position	Goes to cruising state	0.5 sec max
OFF	Turns off	Throttle Position	Goes to inactive state	0.5 sec max
Start Accel	Turns on	Throttle Position	Goes to Accelerating state	0.5 sec max
Maintain Accel	Turns on	Throttle Position	Goes to Accelerating state	0.5 sec max
Running	Turns on	Throttle Position	Goes to Monitor Average Speed	0.5 sec max
Shaft Rotation	Rotation Rate Changes	Throttle Position	To Cruising, Displayed	1 sec max
Fuel Quantity	Entered	Fuel Consumption	Displayed	10 sec max
Avg Spd Rqst	Turns on	Avg Spd	Displayed	1 sec max
Start Trip	-	-	-	No time-critical output
Start Msrd Mile	-	-	-	

Figure 5-10. *Timing specification table*

Requirements Dictionary

Part of the requirements model is the requirement dictionary. As simple as it might sound, the requirement dictionary is essential in overall product development. The requirement dictionary works not only as a communication protocol that unifies all the different languages across various engineering disciplines involving product development, but also it works as a quick checklist of various functions building the product. It also acts like a table of contents for Data or Control Flow diagrams. Please see Figure 5-11.

Definitions, States, Units	Data/Control
Accel = Measure Vehicle Acceleration\Units: Miles per hour per sec.	D
Activate = Driver's cruise control activation command\ Two values: ON, OFF.	C
Avg Spd = Calculated Average Trip Speed\ Units: Miles per hour.	D
Avg Spd Rqst = Driver's request to display the average speed.	C
Cruise Commands = Maintain Speed, Select Speed, Start Accel, Maintain Accel, Resume, ON, OFF, Cancel.	C
Shaft Rotation = Input pulse stream corresponding to angular rotation of drive shaft\ Units:Arbitrary angular unit per pulse.	D
Fuel Quantity = Entered value of fill-up fuel quantity\ Units: Gallons	D

Figure 5-11. *Requirement dictionary*

Architectural Model

If you combine the architectural template with DFD0 and CFD0 for this example we can call the resultant Architectural Flow Diagrams. Consequently, if the architectural template is combined with DCD and CCD, we can call it Architectural Context Diagram. Please see Figures 5-12 and 5-13.

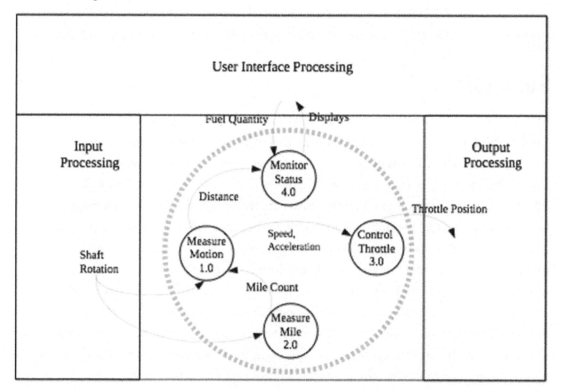

Figure 5-12. *System architecture with an integrated data flow visualization*

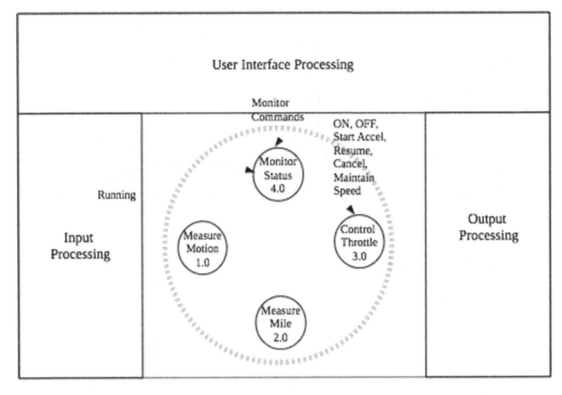

Figure 5-13. *System architecture with an integrated control flow visualization*

Summary

Although the example we discussed here was very simple and only represented a very small portion of an actual product, by only looking at the relative amount of paper works being generated for this small product, you realize how much work needs to be done before even starting to write a line of code or soldering a wire on your board. The main dilemma is how an engineer can write down the details of a project so well without knowing what the end product will look like. Remember the cone of uncertainty that we discussed in the earlier chapters? You can squeeze the base of the cone with the help of the requirements model but you can never diminish the cone to be a straight line. This means that changes are always inevitable anywhere outside of the fairyland of classical methods. The classical methods of project development are stiff against changes because their outlook is idealistic. This attitude toward changes can cause unwarranted reactions from the developers against changes. In the worst cases, either the developers ignore the change or they mistreat it but never welcome them.

Bibliography

[1] Hartley, Derek J., and Imtiaz A. Pirbhai. *Strategies for Real-Time System Specifications.* New York: Dorset House Publishing Co. Inc., 1988, p. 283.

CHAPTER 6

Process Architecture

In the previous chapter we discussed a practical problem for the requirements model of an automobile monitor and control system. Because having a requirement model is one of the major parts that Scrum lacks, it is deemed necessary to discuss the problem through the Hatley and Pirbhai method first. However, we know that the paperwork era that used to make us feel productive is long gone. The majority of design package software offers services that make you able to create and organize the design documents. On the other hand, we all know going into a project with no clear development plan will let the tools dictate the methods. For example, some of the MBD tool manufacturers allow you to use parallel programing for some of your specific applications and some vendors can't offer tools with this capability. If you try to choose your tools first, then you have to fit your architecture to match the tool's capabilities.

Although Hatley and Pirbhai's method is out of date, their philosophy still carries a powerful force that can bring back a dead project to life, rescue troubled ones, and create fine architectures that can mature beautifully. This beauty is envisioned in a systematic and constant development growth, resulting in functional parts meeting all the requirements with minimum waste spent in resource utilization.

In this chapter we look at the entire process of developing the same system through a different approach. This approach as we discussed before includes a very important and decisive part. Although the requirements model cannot answer all the problems that a real-time system development will face, it will answer the most important questions. What does it take to have a cost-effective product that meets all the requirements? How don't we get lost in the complexity of our own product? How do we make hard architectural decisions and how do we back up our decisions with facts? How can we create an architecture that can be utilized in other product development processes? How should we keep track of things necessary for the product and to prioritize functions and processes in both product and development? We leverage this powerful tool and add even more powerful tools to it such as V-Model and DFM in a structured Scrum environment so the product would have a sharp take-off at the concept phase and

© Mohsen Mirtalebi 2017
M. Mirtalebi, *Embedded Systems Architecture for Agile Development*,
https://doi.org/10.1007/978-1-4842-3051-0_6

smooth landing at the manufacturing phase. The requirement model will address the co-location problem in Scrum and a host of other issues because now you have a tool that lets you communicate effectively and accurately with your colleagues around the globe. On the other hand, the "potentially shippable product" concept will address the lack of the requirements model's flexibility in the face of process/product changes. All these efforts stem from the base of requirements model leading to a functional and flexible system architecture that is now interlocked with the development efforts.

Since now we have decided to follow structured Scrum over CPD, we need to rephrase some terminologies. One of these terms is the word "phase" that is the reminiscent of the good old phase-gate method of development. We'd like to replace this word with a more Agile friendly word, "release." If you remember from Chapter 3, we introduced the release concept in the modified V-Model structure. Therefore from here on we will call each product phase a product release referring to the same concept of product release in Scrum. Please see an example of a traditional V-Model in a modern Agile framework in Figure 6-1.

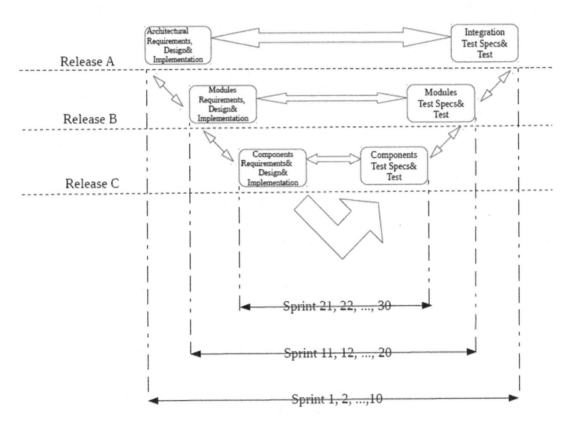

Figure 6-1. *A reminder of V-Model in a Scrum environment*

Consider that more than half a million patent applications were filed in the United States last year, of which maybe only a handful of have made it on the manufacturing stage successfully. If you are the owner of a hi-tech start-up company who needs money for her/his product and services, the investors and bankers require you to demonstrate your ability of starting and managing your company successfully by providing them with a business plan, grant application, and so forth. In a large corporation, the marketing personnel for starting a new product are required to follow a similar method to be able to fund the project, and so are the professors who like to submit grant applications for their research.

The inspiration for dividing the project into major components is a product of a logical process that is deep-rooted in human logics. Since the phase-gate concept of CPD is inspired by this process and not based on project management techniques, it will never suffer from the lashes of time. It also can apply to any facets of life, let it be arts, business, research, banking, manufacturing, and so on. What this means is that new idea development should be the first phase of the development process. Although our method here does not follow a phase-gate process distinctively, we'll let the spirit of it flow through our process. As a result the ideas hereafter are organized in a CPD fashion. You might recall from our earlier discussion that the first phase on the CPD was to develop the product concept.

Proof of Concept

A CPD process or any logical process such as CPD that is for developing new ideas starts off with the most important step of the process, which is to conceptualize the idea in a way that would be presentable to the criticizing eyes of the investors, bankers, project stakeholders, government agents, public eyes, and so on. Since we are specifically talking about developing a real-time system a presentable idea is normally conceptualized as a prototype in a phase that is called the proof of concept phase. To show how important this process is, CPD in its phase-gate method has assigned an entire phase to it. However, it is also the most underestimated phase of all CPD phases. The reason why this phase is often underprocessed is that this process can hardly commit to any specific time, budget schedule, process, or guidelines.

Although every project that works based on a CPD framework must complete the proof of concept phase, some projects tend to finish their concept phase stronger than others. By stronger we mean how much of real engineered forms and engineering methods are going to be put in the first prototype of which they can be later recycled in other aspects of development, downstream. This phase is also very important for our structured Scrum framework as it will produce our first "potentially shippable product." Since the proof of concept by itself is a product, as we saw in our modified V-Model, the conceptualization phase should follow the steps in our flat V-Model. Although we have always emphasized creating a proof of concept as close as possible to the form of final product, we know that this is not always possible. Therefore engineering methods, algorithms, simulations, and virtual models are also considered prototypes. But the point I am making here is not to limit your prototyping efforts but to remind you that while you are creating your first prototype, you should have other teams and functions in mind. Because, what you create has used company's resources; therefore what you create in terms of model, engineering efforts, scientific facts, formulas, algorithms, simulations, and test methods to be reused in other phases of development by different teams.

When the developers create prototypes, they normally try to pursue a few different goals with it. One of the misconceptions about the purpose of this phase is that a prototype is to provide the project stakeholders with some visual aids to grasp the concept. But the actual purpose of this phase is to create the theory and all its supporting documents to be transferred to the next phase. A working prototype is also very useful for the development team who would take over the concepts and prototypes from the research team. However in many actual cases, because of the misconception described earlier, the prototypes are not scalable or expandable to the next phases, and they will be disposed of when they serve their sole purpose of demonstrations. Therefore a strong finish for a concept phase is to create and pass on as many documents, developmental tools, software, and hardware as possible to the next phase. This is not possible unless your prototype is relevant to the next phases of development, in form and functions, following homogenous and active product architecture.

This will create a dilemma for CPD-based processes because then the prototyping comes before architectural development. If you assume your prototype is also your product, then you can have architecture before prototyping, because you are going to follow a flat V-Model process (Figure 6-2). But how can you produce architecture without a clear view on what a product looks like? You don't have to know everything about the product in order to lay out a preliminary architectural layer. The MRD implemented in an active architecture utilizing MBD and requirements model allows you to take the first solid steps without knowing the product and the processes involved entirely. You don't have to take these first steps blindfolded either. There are tools and signs along the way. The principles of recycling in methods and resources are the signs. If you are able to recycle your prototype then you are pretty much on the right path to creating an active architecture that will be expandable and scalable to the next phases of development. In the remainder of this chapter we will be discussing the principles of recycling in engineering efforts.

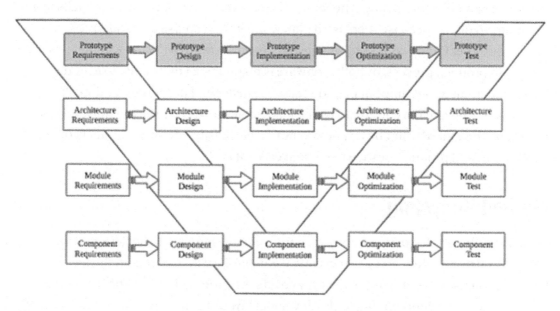

Figure 6-2. *A flat V-Model compared to traditional V-Model*

Hardware Recycling

Unfortunately, unless it contains a cutting edge and propriety technology, most of hardware prototypes nowadays are of little to no value for the next phase of CPD, because no matter how complex they are, they are created for the sole reason of demonstrating the physical aspect of the product. We create the prototypes thinking they can be replaced by other hardware with the same functionalities or they can be easily simulated or animated by the software. Unless the hardware is precisely created to work as a model or template for the next generation of products, they are often of little to no use for the next phases of the same development. In structured Scrum and in the spirit of Agile methods the waste should be contained; therefore the prototypes should be designed to be recycled because the prototype is another release of product.

Software Recycling

During the concept development the researchers not only create original ideas in form of hardware but most importantly create some invaluable intellectual properties expressed in the form of models and algorithms of which both are or can be expressed in software format. Because software seemingly looks easy to scale and expand, then recycling the software should be inherently an uncomplicated task. But we all know that this statement can't be more wrong. The reason the software development always fails to go according to plan is because there is no plan when its first sparks are ignited.

On the other hand, we should change our attitude toward software whether it is used directly in product, process, or both. Software is no longer a commodity like hardware. It carries a tremendous amount of trade secrets, intellectual properties, and wealth of knowledge. Software is a conduit to let the knowledge flow. If we see the software in the right light, then there won't be any option but to let it easily flow from product concept to deployment and product return when it makes a full cycle.

Method Recycling

If you have already decided to have your hardware and software to be designed for recycling purposes, then method recycling would be easy to implement. By now we know that our active architecture not only covers the product but also the processes. At the concept development phase the developers would come up with methods as part of processes for benchmarking and testing the unique software and hardware features. There might be also some special hardware and software tools developed for that purpose in the form of software test cases and hardware test fixtures. The methods and tools for product benchmarking and testing are of a direct use in design, implementation, and manufacturing phases. The test methods can be polished and scaled up or down to be utilized in the succeeding phases, downstream in engineering and manufacturing groups.

Team Dynamics in Concept Release

The team dynamics is also part of product process; hence it should be considered in our active architecture model. In the traditional view of product development it might not seem too relevant but it is, according to DFM principles. As we can also see in an example later in this chapter, that software development is the key in which it creates a common forum among various development departments. The following are only a handful of major players in the embedded system development.

Purchasing Department

Although in many companies purchasing is not considered as part of the core developmental team, what they can bring to the table can surprise you. Let's assume halfway through the prototyping efforts the purchasing team realizes that the manufacturer of our new microprocessor is acquired by another company with the intention of making the new micro obsolete. Now we have to carry out the process of new parts qualification again. If our purchasing team is equipped with software and hardware test methods then we can recycle the software, hardware, and methods used in our old part to qualify the new part. This is part of what makes your development Agile. Again, this is not possible unless you have an active product architecture. Let's remember that active product architecture includes processes too.

Manufacturing Department

You might think these two phases of CPD, concept development and manufacturing, which are on the opposite sides of the development process, have nothing to do with each other – but they do, much more than one might think. What is common between these two phases is the core functionality of the product. In the concept phase a prototype is being created with minimum features to address the core functions and there are some studies or tests performed to estimate the possibility of achieving the core functions. In manufacturing the product is being tested against the same core functions. The level of product attraction and the tests to validate those principle functions is same.

The similarities in the scope of the tests, making the tools, whether to use hardware and/or software platforms, and the methods for carrying out the tests, should be shared between research and manufacturing departments. This tremendously helps to shorten the manufacturing process and eventually shorten the time to market of the product with the least amount of problems and waste in time and money. If we let the manufacturing get exposed to the concept phase, it, along with the purchasing function, can carry materials planning, product distribution, vendor qualifications, and project logistics far ahead of the development schedule. This might seem too early to have everyone involved in development, but the inputs or the lack thereof, from these teams will either make or break your development process. This is something that needs to happen sooner rather than later before the product starts sprinting toward the finish line. This approach also is useful in traditional CPD framework as it provides an early estimate of the product's finished cost, which can facilitate the decision-making process of the stakeholders shortly after the connect phase is completed. The stakeholders' logic is to cut the losses at the earliest time. No need to remind that to achieve all these, we need to unify tools utilized in research and manufacturing. No development framework is more suitable to do the unification but Agile and no tool are more effective in Agile for embedded systems than having an active product architecture developed by MBD and requirements model.

Marketing and Research Departments

We would not discuss the marketing and research engineering role at this time because many companies by default have defined these two departments as the default owners of the concept phase. Marketing is one of the stakeholders and one of the generators of the new ideas in this phase. The research engineering function is to materialize these ideas into prototypes. Therefore the involvement of these two disciplines at this stage is essential. It's worth to mention that, in many companies, the research engineering and marketing constitute one entity.

Scrum and the Concept Release

There is a popular idea among Scrum practitioners that allows the existence of an informal time period that happens at the beginning of the development. This almost open ended and loosely defined duration of development is called sprint zero or in some cases sprint minus one. The purpose of this chunk of time is to allow the stakeholders and developers to get ready for the formal project kickoff milestone. The idea of sprint zero is believed to apply also to the projects with distinct concept phases. It also applies to where there is no prototyping phase allowed, because it is thought that each sprint creates a "potentially shippable product." Bottom line, the applicability of sprint zero depends on whether the developers and stakeholders view a prototype as s potentially shippable product or not. This is the point where Scrum starts to wobble. Since we don't want loose ends in critical applications, we have decided earlier on to consider a prototype a product.

However we can still take advantage of the idea of sprint zero with no time restrictions to be assigned to our prototyping activities. In this case, we can introduce the prototyping phase in our structured Scrum as another product release and then plan accordingly. Structured Scrum is an integral part of creating an active product architecture. The flat V-Model makes the backbone of team dynamics, and it will directly impact the flow of knowledge through our development process including in our product. We should believe processes are initiated form product functions and these functions need an active architecture to flourish. Therefore, without the Scrum framework we cannot architect the processes involved in our development and product. However there is another way and it's the good old way of having distinctive developmental phases such as CPD. I don't recommend going on that route, if you are expecting different results.

An Example of DFM in Action in Concept Release

Let's consider our last example on the Automobile Monitor and Control project. Figure 6-3 illustrates the control diagram of and existing system. The torque (T) from the engine was transferred to the shaft and converted to speed (v). In a new marketing proposal we are required to improve upon the accuracy of the measured speed by creating an algorithm that reads the data provided by the gyroscopes in the airbag system in addition to the traditional method of reading the drive shaft sensors. Figure 6-4 shows the conceptual diagram of the new product. As a note, the gyroscopes are used to calculate the automobile's speed vector as well as GPS data for an accurate displacement measurement in order to calculate a very precise speed value.

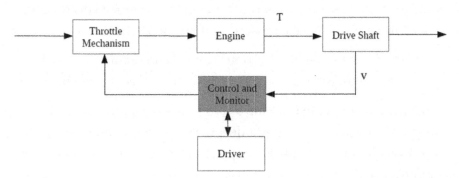

Figure 6-3. *A control diagram for an existing automobile speed measurement system*

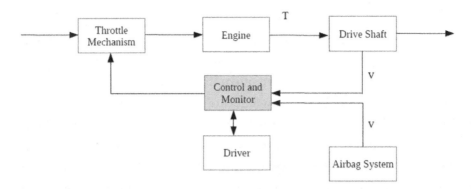

Figure 6-4. *A scaled control diagram*

Since the new algorithm requires additional input pins to accommodate the added data volume, the microprocessor should be replaced by a faster and computationally more powerful microprocessor with additional input pins. Unfortunately the footprint of current microprocessors is not compatible with the new microprocessor; therefore the PCB layout also needs to be changed to facilitate the new required real estate on the existing PCB.

On the other hand, marketing wants to start the project as soon as possible, and the research team can't wait until the control hardware is complete for two reasons: the new hardware needs firmware in order to be tested by the hardware engineers, and there is a 12-week lead time for the delivery of a new microprocessor, including PCB modification and the first hardware prototype build.

There are a few possible scenarios that can be taken into account:

- The research team can work with the existing control boards by kludging some existing parts in order to make the new algorithm and test it on some universal hardware on the bench. (HIL)

- The research team can build a control model and simulate it with the rest of the control software as a plant model on a host computer. (MIL)

- The research team can simulate the control model, generate code from the model, integrate the code into the existing control code, and test it on the existing hardware or just test the software on a general purpose target. (SIL)

As you can see these are just a few different ways to accomplish what we need while waiting on the actual hardware. In all three cases, the existing hardware is very useful but worthless for the next release. In all these three scenarios, all the tools developed to test along the code generated from the core algorithm can be transferred as is to the next phase. The fixtures for testing the hardware can also be transferred to manufacturing engineering to become the base for their functional testing. Also the test cases and codes can be transferred to the engineering and manufacturing team for product verification and validation.

Architecture and Planning

The next phase in the CPD framework is architectural design and planning the project. Since in structured Scrum these activities happen throughout the development, there is no need for a distinctive architecture and planning phase. Rather the project architect can design and implement a simplified version of the product architecture that is fully functional resulting in a "potentially shippable product" at the end. This relates to release A of Figure 6-1 and the first layer of system architecture in Figures 5-12 and 5-13.

The first architectural layer of product will be in its most simple and general form. The essence of simplicity and general form will leave less room for mistakes. If there will be changes introduced to the project later, it wouldn't be about the general form of the project but rather the details of the design. The details would most likely change the components or will modify the existing modules. In any case, if the product architecture is changed it will be easy to absorb the changes because of the modularity of this concept. Again, at this release there is plenty of work for other team members including the design engineers. Figure 6-5 illustrates the flow of work on the second layer of the development process.

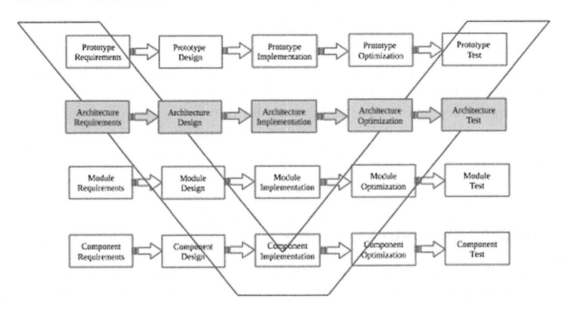

Figure 6-5. *Visualizing the second layer of development in a flat V-Model environment*

Hardware Recycling

The prototype that is being received from the previous release needs to be improved upon. For example, its simulated parts might need slowly to be replaced with the actual parts. With the help of manufacturing engineers, the prototype can work as a test platform for hardware and software functional testing and so forth.

Software Recycling

There might be two types of software that were developed during the concept proofing release: core functional software and the test software for verifying the said functionalities. The separation of software types at this stage might not be as easy as it seems, but during the concept release if we had an eye on the architecture and design release we could have rolled out the software the way it would be easier to be separated. The core functional programs will be used directly in the product architectural layer and the test portion of the software can be utilized for validating the system.

Method Recycling

Similar to the previous release, all the methods can be easily recycled by the current release only if the team intends to design them in such a way to minimize waste with respect to the entire development performance. This again emphasizes having active product architecture.

Team Dynamics

Assuming the same DFM-compliant team is still involved with the product development, they create an appropriate backlog that would highlight the work needed to be done. Since the team dynamic is the same as Scrum, the team creates the backlog items and they also address the responsibilities, objectives, and deliverables.

Modules and Components Releases

We saw how structured Scrum is performed in the more difficult and challenging releases such as concept and architecture releases. Life seems much easier when it gets to merging V-Model and CPD with Scrum for the module and concept releases, because these two releases directly correspond with the design phase of CPD where the product design, implementation, and testing are performed consequentially.

We've observed previously that the module and component releases follow the same trend as the concept and architecture releases. The team dynamics would also look much similar to these releases. Figures 6-6 and 6-7 depict the module and component releases respectively.

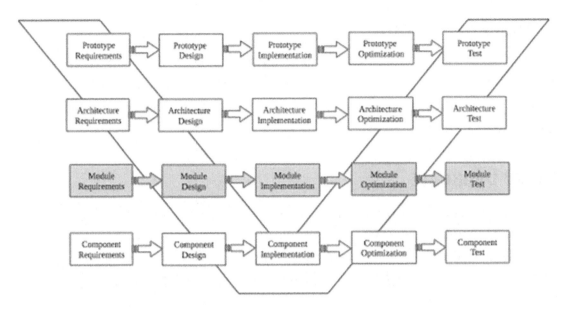

Figure 6-6. *The third phase of a V-Model relative to a flat V-Model*

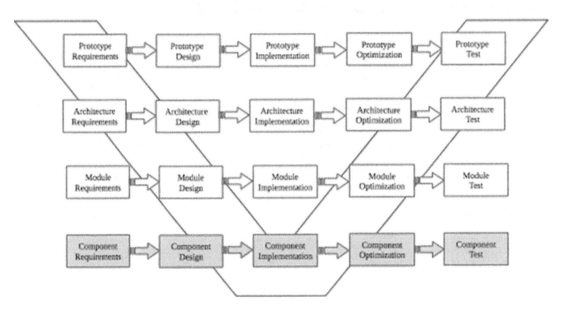

Figure 6-7. *The final phase of a V-Model and flat V-Model*

The Final Release

As we saw in all phases of the traditional V-Model the tasks on a flat V-Model would stay the same. This is not by accident or useless repetition of the same tasks in every release. This is precisely designed to make all the product release processes the same regardless of the progression of product development. This is done by practically departing from the phase-gate concept in product development and applying its logic to every release of product. This is because the structured Scrum, like its counterpart CPD, is disciplined and systematic to product development but more accepting to changes.

This method is developed to ensure the integrity of design is safeguarded with traceability and via minimizing the variability in the development processes. We want to leave the variability only to be introduced by the changes necessary to better our product. On the other hand, it follows an Agile methodology that would keep the team motivated, sensitive, and responsive to the product development changes. As a result, the optimization and V&V phase of CPD is performed at every release. After all, if there is any need for additional optimization and V&V phases, there would not be any need for another product release as traditional Scrum prescribes.

Departing from CPD and Landing on Structured Scrum

In a structured Scrum framework, the CPD process seems to be spread across every sprint, so every one of them carries a small scale but a complete set of CPD. We will describe the layers architecture, which is based on requirements model, in more details in the next chapter. In the meantime, Figure 6-8 shows how layer architecture interacts with structured Scrum.

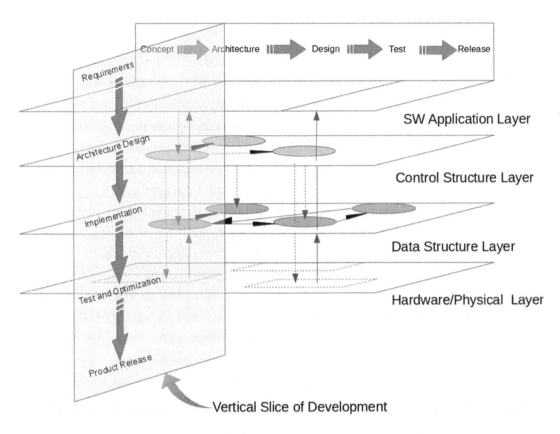

Figure 6-8. *Layer architecture in an Agile development process*

The CPD process runs in two dimensions throughout the development. One is in its classical form during the project time line and it runs horizontally. This is for budget purposes and also communicating with other departments outside of the development group. For example, if the project architect needs to provide a progress report to the finance department s/he could present it to the them in a fashion that they are familiar with. This would have no effect on how the project is being carried out as it only plays as a presentation tool to the outside world.

However, the Agile development process that runs vertically slices through every function involved in the product for the duration of each sprint. The manufacturing tag on the last layer simply applies to the physical layer to denote the concept of product validation, which leads to the release of our potentially shippable product at the end of each sprint. The product validation can be performed at the system, module, or component level together or separately. Let's remember that each hardware or software module or component needs to be verified at least once as long as they are not modified but the product validation needs to be performed at the end of each sprint. Since the product validation in our new Scrum-based process is very similar to product validation in the old CPD-based process in manufacturing, this task can involve the manufacturing engineers. The advantage of involving the manufacturing engineers at this stage of development is countless. Finally, the minimum number of layers of our product can contain Software Application, Control Structure, Data Structure, and Physical layers. However you can add more layers to it depending on your application.

Referring to the example of new product development in Chapter 3, the simplest form of a product in a real-time system might have a minimum number of 21 activities that would touch up on all the named architectural layers. This might represent a very simple project of turning an LED on.

The first row of the activities we see in Figure 6-9 is consistent with all the activities on the architectural layer of the product. If this layer is planned to be finished on one sprint then we could have a potentially shippable product at the end of the same sprint. However the project architect can decide by adding more resources to finish all 21 tasks in one shot on the same sprint. This might sound logical but because of the task dependencies, some tasks can't start before another one is complete. So the resource assignment might be too complicated, which complicates the delivery date as a consequence.

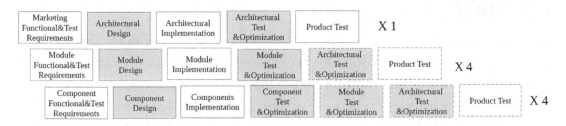

Figure 6-9. *A reminder of flat V-Model in an Agile framework*

Smoke Test

The term "smoke test" is usually used in the software environment and it is a test being performed on a server that builds the product software, anytime there is a new version of code checked into the source control system. Any checked-in code will trigger the build server to build the entire software including incorporating the built firmware for the hardware. This test is completely automatic with a pass-fail criterion, which means at the end of the build process either the build has been successful or the build has failed. The smoke test can be developed further to include the product hardware, which means the product software will be automatically downloaded on the hardware and then the entire product is going to be validated.

Agile Testing

At the end of each row in Figure 6-9 there is a common task occurring every time and it's called "product test." Ideally, this is a test performed with growing cumulative test cases. The growth comes from the fact that at each sprint we are adding more functions and features to our product. We could compare this with a regression testing in software. This is an integral part of sprint activities and if this task is not complete, the sprint is not complete. We can combine this test with a smoke test in order to avoid surprises at the end of the sprint. However this test can also be designed to act as software/hardware black box testing as well as white box testing in addition to regression testing. It is at the discretion of the team to decide. Once the hardware prototype is added, the test will cover both hardware and software. The types and combinations of tests you can carry out are almost limitless. Again, the guidance comes from the active product architecture.

Summary

Scrum has no preferences on what type or sees no interruption from any type of phase-gate frameworks similar to CPD. It can peacefully coexist with traditional methods but it should be in control of development. However, the development management of real-time systems can't accept CPD because the software faction of it is more prone to the changes than a rigid phase-gate method can bear. On the other hand, the firmware in real-time systems due to its criticality needs a firmer and more defined structure than what Scrum can offer for a mixed software-hardware development. Because the real-time system by definition carries critical applications and as a result is under a higher level of scrutiny from various governmental and certification agencies, this and the co-location issue in Scrum has forced us to find a method in between Agile and classical processes. We called it structured Scrum. The underlying principle of structured Scrum of real-time systems is still Agile but to provide both, better communication channels between engineers in different geographical locations and time zones and better traceability, we have inserted the classical method of requirements model. To be compliant with the requirements model we need to form clear product architecture. Because the requirements model is heavily based on paper-based processes, with the introduction of MBD tools we were able to create the foundation of an active product architect that can utilize a layers model.

CHAPTER 7

Layers Model

The layers model of embedded systems architecture is based on model-based design (MBD) to facilitate Agile development. In any development framework we'd like to minimize the development constraints while maximizing the quality of engineering work. This model not only achieves those, but also it reduces the waste incurred during the development. The fundamental of the layers model architecture is based on the fact that engineering principles are not in any kind of conflict with business decisions, and these two can both be aligned with our environmental responsibilities. In fact, how much our development impacts our environment is a sign of how well we have applied the engineering principles to make sound and ethical business decisions. For doing so, the layers model distinguishes between process and product. The fundamental of layers model is based on MBD.

What Is a Model?

As we discussed before, the earliest traces of model-based design comes from the UML program. This is a software tool created by IBM to enable software engineers to define software behavior and its architecture through graphical representations rather than in textual format. There are many companies whose software tools carry various capabilities that allow design engineers to create system architecture and develop, simulate, and test systems and codes. These tools are ideal for an Agile environment because they eliminate unnecessary documents by merging requirements, design, and implementations phases of development. This is the main reason that a model is also known as executable specification, which acts as both a software program and a design document. Although there are many advantages in utilizing programming models such as facilitating the design and also design validation and verification (V&V), requirements traceability, a much shorter integration phase, higher-quality end product, faster time to market, reduced waste in developmental resources, and so forth, the tool cannot

163

© Mohsen Mirtalebi 2017
M. Mirtalebi, *Embedded Systems Architecture for Agile Development*,
https://doi.org/10.1007/978-1-4842-3051-0_7

guide us how to lay out our architectural model, nor will it tell us how to decompose the requirements into functional software and hardware units. It does not tell us how to organize our software modules, and most importantly it doesn't show us in what order to develop and implement these modules for minimizing the waste. In a much larger scale, the tool cannot guide us on how to merge hardware and software functionalities in an embedded system development so our process and product become the most efficient.

This is because a model is only a graphical representation of a system in terms of its static and dynamic behavior with respect to its surroundings of which can also be represented as a model. The best a programming model can do is in a HIL case where it can model a real-world scenario to simulate a physical system. Nevertheless, a model can be a very strong tool to control a physical system in a predictable manner. For example, a CAD model can be materialized into a physical model by a 3D printing machine or a control algorithm model into a C code to be downloaded into a target microprocessor. But none of these means that we have achieved our business goals. Let's not forget that the difference between an engineering firm and a toolmaking shop is in efficiency.

However, the most important advantage of creating models is their capabilities to not only represent a product but also a process. This is a unique advantage that the new age computerized tools have brought us. Before computers, the products were represented by concept prototypes and processes through diagrams on papers. The MBD has introduced this new but very useful concept of an "executable specification" that a model can represent a product while it can specify the processes involved in making the product. For our example, a requirements model can be identified as a process model that can be embedded into a product architectural model and so forth. A requirement model can organize our activities in breaking down the product into modules and components while at the same time acting like glue, holding all the product and process components together.

Process and Product Models

A developmental framework from a grand view consists of two major categories: product and process. The requirements model directly relates to the product portion of the project by organizing activities around the product development such as product architecture, task management, scheduling, and so on. It will also highlight the necessary processes for us. MBD is able to address the needs of both product and process by providing models. A component model depicting a control algorithm is a product model, and a module holding these components together can be considered a process model. The idea of process is abstract enough that it can have any product components and activities under its wings, whether its hardware, software, or manufacturing models activities. Process models are similar to integration or architectural models; they define how product models interact with each other. [1]

Let's assume you have a team of 18 firmware engineers who are responsible for developing control algorithms for your solid state transformer (SST) to be sold in the automotive market. The product has three major units: a bidirectional rectifier, dc-dc converter, and an inverter. You equally distribute your engineers among these three functional development teams and require them to kickstart the development to initiate all three developments simultaneously. There is no way on earth you can start three highly correlated developments at the same time without creating massive waste unless you have a clear picture of the system architecture in mind. Even though if you opt to start the three developments sequentially rather in parallel, the lack of architecture will directly impact the quality of your work, time to market, development resources, customer satisfaction, and finished product cost.

But where does the clear picture of architecture come from? If you remember, when we talked about Cone of Uncertainty, I argued that the more time spent at the design stage the narrower the cone gets for the rest of the development process; hence the clearer and faster the image of product architecture will emerge. We discussed these before we brought up the concept of Agile development. With Agile we won't have phases of product; we will have a product that starts with lesser features and as the development progresses, it will be loaded with more features.

Going back to our SST product and our 18-member team, let's assume we have a clear architectural road map in front of us. Each product module is being developed simultaneously and according to the architecture. Let's assume these control units are also functional as an isolated unit. The rectifier unit performs well with our HIL system. All the data from our validation test indicates the design is sound. The same thing happens with the other two units. Let's also assume all these designs and implementations arrive at the same time so there is no waste of development time while waiting for a unit to be completed. Do you think we are done? The answer is this: far from it. Now we have to make sure all these three units are glued together seamlessly and function flawlessly as one major unit. This is where the process model comes to rescue.

A product's process model, which is also an MBD model, facilitates the integration of all these individual units into what we like to call our product. The beauty of process model is that it is purely product based unlike the process models used in the project management. It is absolutely architecture dependent as it will not even come to existence without it. Finally, it will not require us to have a fixed sequential or parallel development process. It will give you a significant amount of flexibility that you are able to mix and match models, processes, resources, and tools, enabling you to reshuffle, add, and remove any items or resources related to the development.

So far, we have realized the development for our embedded system product requires a control layer, but what we failed to see is the big elephant in the room. As engineers, we are so occupied with the algorithms and functions we sometimes are not able to see the massive amount of data that is being manipulated across our product. The data is the main ingredient of the glue in our process model. Once we know how the data flows, we know the system architecture. The data is purely in a software form. This is the main reason software is the main ingredient of modern embedded systems architecture and the nightmare we are facing day by day. Therefore the process model is more important than your product model. Given, the product model here is the functional models containing the control algorithms. This level of importance comes from the fact that functional codes and control algorithms make up a tiny portion of the amount of code written for an embedded system. Consequently, the process model is from the architecture mode and the architecture model is submerged in the data layer. Unfortunately, people who know data don't know control, and the ones who know control don't know data. If you let the data people develop the process model the product function would suffer, and if you let the control people develop the process model the product and development will become inefficient for the remaining life of that product. So the process model provides a unique environment to let these two very different expertises to come together and design the system that we'd like to call a system architecture.

Product's Process Model

The process of designing the product model is defined by the requirements model. We can choose any other way to define products' functional models but the requirements model will create an environment that invites the data people to collaborate more closely with the product functions. The requirements model also adds the flexibility to the glue in case of scope and on-the-fly design changes. Remember, every product is unique and unknown at the beginning, according to the Cone of Uncertainty.

Since a model-based design is considered an executable specification, following a requirements model will perfectly shape the MBD activities combining requirement, design, and implementation phases at the same time. Although there are some MBD vendors who can equip you with tools for mechanical, electrical, and software models under the same modeling environment, it is not necessary to model everything as long as MIL, SIL, and HIL are performed in such a way that they can validate the product and process models. The flexibility of the requirement model is highly noted here when we slowly replace the simulated parts with the actual released software or hardware modules and components.

The product model as the requirement model has outlined its boundaries, comprised of two hierarchical branches, data and control. This is because this is the first opportunity we give the data people to have their inputs into design, resulting in a tightly integrated data system with control algorithms. This also prevents the control people from avoiding developing the system in a bottom-up fashion, which goes directly against the core principles discussed here. There are a tremendous amount of disadvantages in designing a system in this manner, which I will let you learn by experience and see the results.

In a Simulink environment, there are two types of wire connections between the design elements, signals, and parameters. Signals are time-variant lines of data flow that change values with time. Parameters are the time-invariant values. Signals are analogous to data flow and parameters to control signals.

However, unlike many CAD vendors, so far none of the MBD tool vendors have provided layering mechanisms in their environment. The two main required layers in an MBD environment are control and data flow layers. This will separate the data flow from the control and avoid unnecessary complexity in design. It also greatly helps to scale the models when the system becomes more complex. It later will become vital in debugging and troubleshooting the system.

In Figure 7-1, the data and control layers represent the core functionality of our system. The data and control signals from the user interface or, in other words, the application layer will target the corresponding control and data structure layers. From Figure 4-4, the control signals are noted as dashed arrow lines and data signals are indicated in solid arrow lines. The user interface module of our architecture carries command – in this case, control signals to the control layer and sometimes to the physical layer. The control layer then processes and carries the control command to the data and physical layers. Nowadays some physical layers command the data and control layers also, but this is the root cause of many system security breaches; therefore there is no dashed arrow line from the physical layer to the control and data layers shown here. Instead there are modules on the control layer that control other modules in this layer.

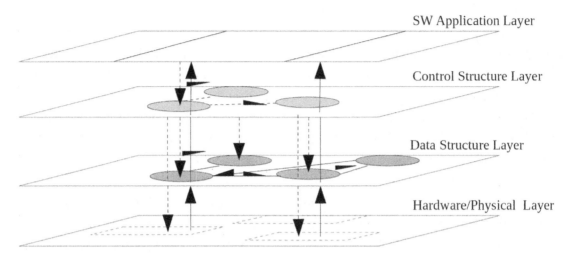

Figure 7-1. *An example of embedded system's architectural layers*

For embedded systems with smart sensors, which are computationally autonomous subsystems, this architecture still applies since the control and data layers of smart sensor systems can be placed on the corresponding system layers. The communication protocol between a subsystem control layer and other control modules however are more elaborated due to physical distance between the processors but makes no difference how they are presented on the control abstraction layer.

Since the layers are common across all the architectural modules mentioned in Figure 4-3, the system's input and output processing will interface with the respective hardware components. Some data and control signals might have a final destination of user interface for monitoring and user processing purposes. If you have noticed the solid lines on the first layer in Figure 7-1, it resembles that of Figure 4-3, the architectural model of the system. Please also note that how each layer is carefully isolated from the other ones. The control layer has one direction, dashed arrow line to lower layers but the data layer has a solid arrow line drawn to every layer in each direction except the physical layer. This is because with having a dedicated data layer for our architectural model, we can handle the data flow for all layers on the data layer. However there are some solid data lines going to some modules on the control layer. This is because oftentimes to let a control algorithm of one module decide what path to take, we need a secondary set of data to provide to the control module to facilitate that.

Like modules and components in the requirements model, product models don't address task scheduling, system interfacing, hardware-software mapping, mass data handling, system requirements, and so forth. The product model, instead, is to help the developers to define, design, simulate, and test algorithms and concepts.

Development Process Model

Models at module and component levels deal with product functions and features; however at the architecture level, models deal with activities, scopes, and marketing requirements also. A process in simple words is a group of activities to develop a real-time system. In our case the architectural portion of requirements model, the integration part of implementation, testing segments of manufacturing, the debugging part of optimization, and the V&V phase and the troubleshooting of deployment are all activities that can utilize MBD tools. At this time, however, there is no MBD tool vendor that offers a development process model due to the size and complexity of these processes, which also require business expertise. However the layer architectural model is aware of these complexities and is designed in such a way that allows the architectural model to easily embed into the existing development processes. As a matter of fact the model is designed specifically with an eye on such processes.

While various engineers, whether they are software or hardware engineers, are developing each portion of the system, the project architect, and the team under the structured Scrum discipline put pieces of the systems together to deliver each version of a potentially shippable product under certain product releases. All these activities are part of the product development process.

A process or architecture model must be able to fully address the following. These items are directly correlated to the items in the requirements model at the architectural level:

- Product Features Scopes and Interfaces

- Data Dictionary and Data Management

- Task Scheduling and System Performance

- Hardware-Software Mapping and Interface Management

- Safety-Critical Functionalities

- V&V and Optimizations

- System Integration and Testing

- Manufacturing

In the following figure, Figure 7-2, each aspect of the product development has its own process, utilizing a fast V-Model system and architectural activities based on the requirements model of that specific segment of product development. We have discussed the details of these processes before in earlier chapters. However if any of these processes follow the same development process, the use of MBD is absolutely crucial to the well-being of the development process in terms of cost and time. This is because the MBD will arm the engineers with a powerful tool that unifies all the tools and consequently activities across the development process from development to manufacturing. This by itself is the definition of an Agile process, and Agile processes are created to cut waste and optimize project resources by introducing uniform methods and tools. Some business tool vendors have become aware of this market demand on uniform processes and developed Scaled Agile Framework (SAFe). The problem with these tools is that the focus is primarily on business development rather than product development, putting the product function at risk, especially for the embedded systems that are often designed to carry out critical missions. The other issue that one can run into is the complexity and weight of SAFe tool becomes so heavy that maintaining the system requires as many resources as the product development. This is the same problem that CPM and CPD ran into when the system became so heavy to carry and eventually collapsed under its own weight. In theory there is a likely possibility that a Scales Agile Framework becomes so big that it becomes practically an anti-Agile entity.

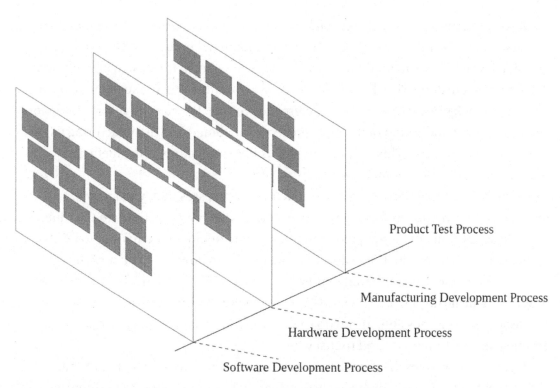

Product Test Process

Manufacturing Development Process

Hardware Development Process

Software Development Process

Figure 7-2. *Scaling up Agile to cover all the processes involved in the product development*

The scaling of the framework happens in an organic way, meaning as unique as each product is, the architecture becomes unique and so does the scaled framework resulting in avoiding unnecessary activities in the product development. We will let the product, through architecture, dictate the development processes. For example, let's imagine you have the product line that is developed and manufactured in the United States, and the same product with some minor changes (let's say cost reduction and less features) is going to be developed and manufactured in another country. The SAFe for these almost identical products would be greatly different because two countries would have certainly different governmental policies, certification processes, design and manufacturing cultures, resource planning, and many other differences. This is why every product is unique so let's not make the illusion of one-can-fit-all real.

Therefore the layer model creates an additional product development process layer on top of other product layers. So far we have unified the hardware, software, and manufacturing developmental processes by requiring these developments to follow the same tools; MBD; same development processes; Structured Scrum; and same architectural development process, the requirements model.

If you are coming from a design background you might question how manufacturing processes can follow the same processes as developmental processes. That's a very valid question if you believe in building walls. The popular belief in the design environment is that once you are done with the design you throw it over the wall to the manufacturing. We'll let them figure out how to manufacture the product. We have discussed this before and this is not an indication of the Agile process even though the manufacturing follows closely an Agile process. This is like saying it's ok to manufacture a very inefficient product with very efficient manufacturing processes.

If you have experience with the manufacturing processes then you know once a manufacturing engineer is faced with a new design s/he has to go through the same CPD phases of concept, design, implementation, and deployment in order to be able to manufacture the product. The devilish detail in this is how soon you are willing to get the manufacturing involved to prevent wastes and improve the quality of your product. Realistically it would be wise to get the manufacturing involved as early on in the design stages as possible. If you do so then the product test process would be the ground showing how ready and robust your design is.

Figure 7-2 illustrates the points discussed so far. Each process, whether they are software or hardware of manufacturing development process, follows a harmonized flat V-Model in a Structured Scrum framework synched by a product test process. The test will provide not only feedback to the design and product function, it also shows how effective our development processes are. Additionally it creates a cadence among all teams and team members involved.

MBD Tools

Whether you have a complex system of highly nonlinear differential equations that model the dynamics of a physical system for your plant model or you are after implementing a system of cascaded state machines for your control layer of your product, the MBD tools are there to help you solve, simulate, and implement them for the physical world. Like CAD tools, the MBD tools create a virtual model of the system you are designing as well as allowing you to generate functional codes that can be implemented on the hardware to carry out your applications for your final product. In addition, the MBD tools let you optimize your overall system in an unprecedented way as you develop your product.

It is wrongfully believed that the automatic code generation part adds some overhead to the overall size of your code but if that's even true, these tools compensate that by shorting the path from design to implementation and integration. They also make the overall system very efficient by preventing redundancies, unifying coding styles, and using robust coding methods. All in all, utilizing MBD guarantees a faster time to market for your product that otherwise would take much longer to achieve due to reworks.

Among all the benefits that MBD brings us, rapid prototyping is the first one that we get to experience. We discussed various configurations of MBD in rapid prototyping such as MIL, SIL, and HIL. Figure 7-3 shows some of these configurations. In this case PSIM, which is a power electronics modeling and simulation software, either converts the model to code and then code is being downloaded onto a target hardware to be utilized for a hardware-in-the-loop test, or there is hardware adaptor that takes the model and then it will be interfaced with the rest of the hardware loop.

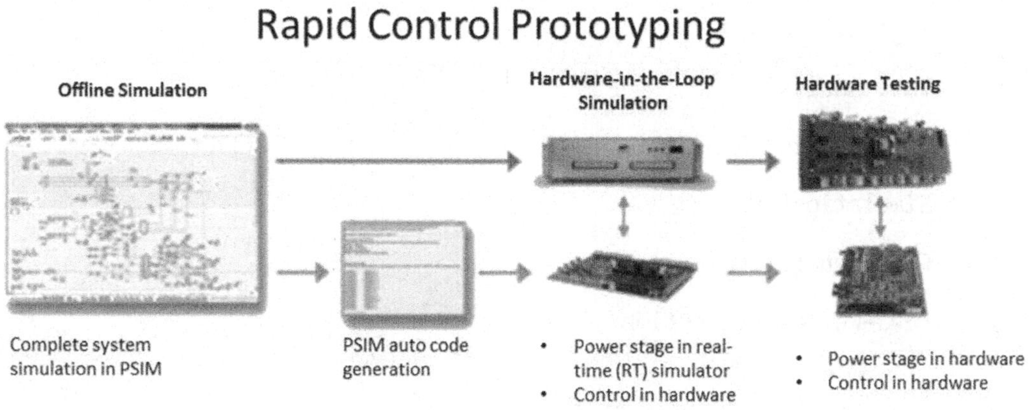

Rapid Control Prototyping

| Offline Simulation | | Hardware-in-the-Loop Simulation | Hardware Testing |

| Complete system simulation in PSIM | PSIM auto code generation | • Power stage in real-time (RT) simulator
• Control in hardware | • Power stage in hardware
• Control in hardware |

Figure 7-3. *Different stages of in-the-loop processes from MIL to HIL (Courtesy of Typhoon HIL)*

MBD Utilization Steps

The first step in model-based design does not start with drawing the models. It starts with understanding the model's requirements. The requirements model method that we discussed earlier in detail, specifically at the PSPEC and CSPEC level, can translate the requirements to models almost in a one-to-one relationship. In other words, the requirements model can be fully implemented in an MBD environment. This is because the majority of functional specifications are either in mathematical or conditional form.

Although model-based design methodologies and tools are still at their infancy to be able to cover all the needs of a real-time system development with sophistication but they still can address the majority of the developers' needs.

A model in a model-based design environment is considered an "**executable specification.**" This is because a model can gather all the following information in one place:

- System-Level Architecture

- Hierarchical Structures

- Graphical Representation

- Interactive Product specification (place mouse over element to "hover" over element and see information regarding element)

- Multidomain Functional Definitions with One Common Method

- Algorithm Design

- Data Analysis

- Highlighting Dependencies

- Simulation

- Code Generation

- Real-World Interaction

Layer Model and MBD

After the mathematical and logical form of the requirements model is designed as a model, it then can be simulated and tested to verify its functionality. Testing the design at model level is very important as it shortens the length of time at integration into the final product. It also creates meaningful test values for benchmarking the product and to be used later in V&V, optimization, and even manufacturing tests and product return. Figure 7-4 illustrates how MBD is used in a traditional V-Model. Since this is a common practice among firmware developers utilizing MBD in a traditional V-Model environment, the deployment of MBD in a flat V-Model and Structured Scrum framework is even easier and comes as more natural since MBD is keen to early and often V&V tests. But this is not the end of the story. The tool can be utilized at every stage of the product life cycle from requirements development to manufacturing and beyond. Consequently, this makes the layer model highly organic to the embedded systems development processes.

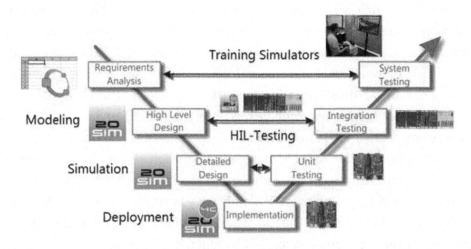

Figure 7-4. *In-the-loop solutions for various phases on V-model (Courtesy of Control Lab)*

In addition, since all the stages of the V-Model are developed in the same tool, they can be summarized and manifested as a unit of the development process. This is absolutely an Agile process by definition and in accordance to DFM. This is the tool that marries the CPD framework to Agile methodology and eliminates various steps that were previously required by the CPD and V-Model processes. Now we can see how layer models facilitate the development process among various teams that otherwise could not find a common ground to stand on and start communicating with each other.

The proof-of-layer model practicality is that there are MBD vendors who also make hardware and software that not only are used in the research environment but the very same tools are used by the development team as well as in the manufacturing environments. We need to take advantage of the fact that there are tool vendors who have already recognized the unification need and they have commercially available products utilized among various engineering departments. All we need to do is to let our products tell us how and when to use these tools. The layer model embedded in an Agile method does just that.

Figure 7-5 shows only the product side of the story, but by now we know the number of layers on top of the product are greater than what is shown in this figure. I avoid crowding the picture in order to facilitate your understanding of it. The layer model utilizing the requirements model tells us what is needed to be designed and implemented in the first Sprint. The start of the Sprint is marked clearly by the arrow as "Sprint One." Therefore what you see is one unit of Sprint from concept to design, implementation, test, and release. In this Sprint the architectural layer is designed; the major modules for the data and control layers are identified and implemented; and either a dummy hardware or MIL, SIL, CHIL, and HIL is utilized to implement the design. Then we either run the prototype in a purely simulated environment, run on the target hardware, or anything in between. At the test stage of this Sprint the Product Test Process will be performed in order to make sure manufacturing is also following the rest of development. This image is the unification of all developmental processes and a true Agile framework by definition. At the end of any Sprint you will have a potentially shippable product that is tested. The test provides design and manufacturing feedback by giving you a taste of a vertical slice of the product. Bon Appetit!

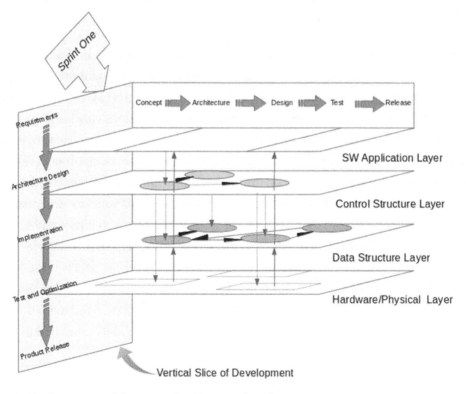

Figure 7-5. *Layers architecture for Scrum development*

In the second Sprint the modules are developed more in details and another test is being performed at the end. The progression of details development follows the same path shown in Figure 4-15 following a requirements model utilizing MBD tools. The core idea here is that you draw a very narrow and continuous path from the user interface to the hardware with the minimum product functionality and featurization. As the development advances, this line becomes bolder and broader until it covers the entire product features and functionality. This incremental delivery of values to the customer creates cadence among the team members.

As we will discuss in the next section, the layers model also is very compatible with the existing MBD build processes, as you can assign to different teams the data and control layers that can work hand in hand during each sprint. The layers model provides the path of what functionalities are required for the current Sprint and how data and control layers interact with each other. This is a huge win for the layers model since we know as the system developed the functionalities become much more complicated; hence going back and redesigning the earlier modules is hugely costly and time consuming. The MBD build process also comes naturally to the added manufacturing process layer because many manufacturing methods have already adopted some derivation of the Agile framework in one form or another: as an example, lean manufacturing comes to mind.

MBD's Build Process

As soon as the requirements for a function in the system are ready we can develop the model. This is as simple as knowing the problem before starting to solve it. There is no complicated logic in this process and there are no shortcuts. Following an Agile process gives us no excuse to bypass the requirements model development. However in a process utilizing MBD as a tool, we can get creative and combine the requirements and design documents with the actual function we are trying to design.

Another tremendous benefit of using MBD is that we can visualize the performance of our system before it is physically realized. For that we not only need our algorithm model but also a behavioral model that would together create a test bed for our design. The behavioral models contain various parts of which one is the plant models. If you are designing a cruise control system for an existing power train system, the model of power train system is a plant model for your cruise control model. These two models then make a behavioral model.

The behavioral model then can be simulated in addition to individual function models to reduce the design flaws and improve functionality and performance of the system. Although there is some skepticism regarding how well a model can represent a physical system, the models can be used for benchmarking for the future physical system, to say the least. However a model is as good as its designer. An incomplete model will generate incomplete results.

After designing your function in a form of a model, you can either integrate it with other functional models and then integrate with the rest of the system, or you can individually integrate it with the system. At this stage you also have the option to do HIL, MIL, and SIL.

Furthermore, we can generate automatic code from the model and then integrate it into the system. At this stage again, we can perform another set of HIL and SIL tests to improve the design and generate more benchmarking. Please note the behavioral models are one that model the system under development as a black box. The only known elements of black box systems are the inputs and outputs because we can control the input and measure the output. There are regression and mathematical tools that are able to express the black box's behavior in mathematical forms without knowing what really is inside the box. For example, Matlab provides a toolbox called System Identification that would just do that. Please see Figure 7-6.

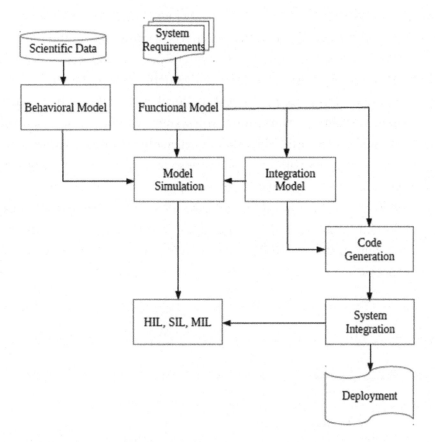

Figure 7-6. *A build model for MBD*

MBD in Layers Model

No matter how we look at the real-time system development, the first step is to create a requirements model. From an architectural standpoint, the models that are in the form of components and modules must be placed in a system that might be composed of various platforms whether in the form of hardware or software. This means that your system architecture comprises both hardware and software functionaries but at the same time agnostics to either platforms. Then as we discussed before, the system simulation can be carried out in many different fashions of which HIL and SIL are among the most popular tests. In our case any of the in-the-loop methods are not restricted to one platform. They test architectural functionalities regardless of their platforms.

The system analysis then will follow to provide feedback to the task scheduler in our system software, individual performance reports of components and modules, and the effectiveness of the assumed architecture with respect to timing specification. All these will provide us with a massive amount of invaluable data that would empower us to better our design while keeping the costs of development down. In a structured Scrum environment utilizing a layers model, the system is complete at the end of each Sprint but it contains less features. The product will acquire more and more features and functionalities as it grows with time. The project architect is in charge of the process model and then the engineers are in charge of the product model. This will empower the product architect to act as a program manager consolidating responsibilities and making faster decisions. Earlier in this chapter we introduced the process and product models. Figure 7-7 illustrates a modified version of Figure 7-6, which is tailored for our flat V-Model process.

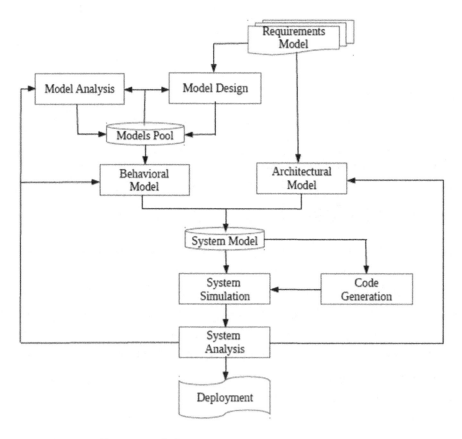

Figure 7-7. *MBD in flat V-Model*

MBD Platforms

There are many platforms that can provide you with tools ranging from model design to simulation and implementations that cover many aspects of the product from software to simulating mechanical parts. Simulink and LabView are the most used modeling software from Mathworks Inc. and National Instruments Inc. respectively.

In addition, in our examples we referenced graphs from various different companies whose logo is presented on the pictures. You can consult with their corresponding websites in order to inquire about more information. In many cases, the graphical user interfaces seemingly look similar. For example, in LabView the graphical user interface looks like that in Figure 7-8.

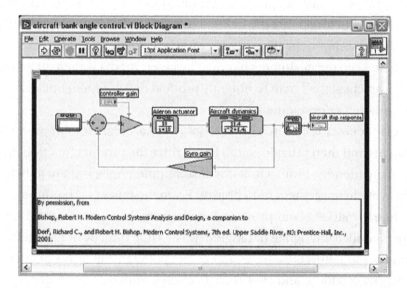

Figure 7-8. *NI sample MBD in its native visual language, LabView. (Courtesy of National Instruments Corporation)*

For Simulink samples, please visit: http://www.mathworks.com.

Summary

Engineering documentations are of grave importance even more so for embedded systems because most of these devices are for mission-critical applications. However, for various reasons, engineers are reluctant to develop or still more hesitant to maintain these documents. Additionally, creating and maintaining documents are time consuming and takes valuable engineering resources away when these resources can contribute directly to the product development. The layers model with the help of MBD creates a long overdue shortcut to combine what is necessary with what is functional.

Aside from documentations, requirements traceability is also another important aspect of engineering work that is not only used for the internal operations to keep the checks and balances but also for product certifications and governmental compliance processes. But let's not forget that the main benefit of requirements traceability is to keep the product development aligned with what is absolutely necessary for the product and at the end to keep the customers happy. The layers model is there just to do that by providing a practical road map to not only product development but also processes involved in a product's development.

The layers model started from what is absolutely necessary for our product to meet the requirements and then provide a path to organize the product functionality in such a way that is Agile friendly. From a functional standpoint, Agile is there to help the quality of the work in implementation phases. From the business standpoint, it's there to facilitate time to market of our product. Finally, from the environmental standpoint, Agile is there to reduce intangible or tangible wastes that directly or indirectly contribute to exploitation of our natural resources and create pollutants in terms of material waste, low-quality products, and overusage of energy sources as a result of inefficient developmental processes and products.

Bibliography

[1] Schätz, Bernhard, Alexander Pretschner, Franz Huber, and Jan Philipps. "Model-Based Development of Embedded Systems." *OOIS Workshops* (2002).

CHAPTER 8

MBD and Requirements Model

In this chapter we will bring a practical example of an automobile cruise control that we discussed earlier in the requirements modeling chapter. The steps of developing a requirement model will follow in parallel with its MBD equivalent. The MBD models then will be divided into two categories: product and process models. The product model will follow the PBS and the process model will benefit from the architectural template, timing specification, data dictionary, and more.

From the previous chapters we know that the requirements model starts with DCD and CCD, which defined the boundaries of the system architecture. To avoid unnecessary complications, we used a very simple cruise control example. In Figure 8-1, the two top figures show the DCD and CCD respectively and the bottom figure the architectural template.

© Mohsen Mirtalebi 2017
M. Mirtalebi, *Embedded Systems Architecture for Agile Development*,
https://doi.org/10.1007/978-1-4842-3051-0_8

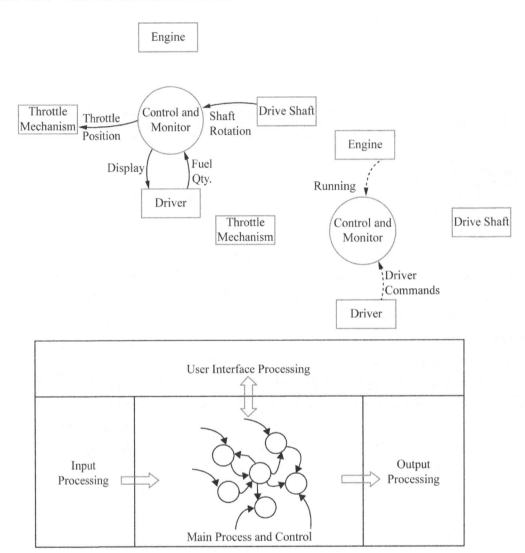

Figure 8-1. *An overview of high-level functional specs, DCD and CCD, in conjunction with system architecture*

Combining the DCD and CCD diagrams within an architectural template in a MBD environment will produce a model that is presented below. As it is evident, there is a one-to-one relation between our requirements model and our MBD model.

The highlighted area in Figure 8-2 represents the system we are trying to design. It contains all four major modules of our architectural template. As you can see, the wire connectors represent two types of intermodule connections, data and control. Although Simulink lacks providing separate layers for control and data, we can still distinguish between these two by creating data and control buses. Any signal that is labeled as control, status, state, and monitor are all with a control nature and the rest are data based.

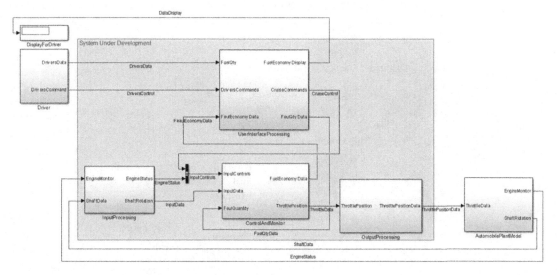

Figure 8-2. *How architecture and specifications come together in an MBD environment*

The input and output processing modules can have an architecture of their own, depending on their level of complexity and sophistication. Various types of database schemas, handshaking mechanisms, hardware-software interfaces, and much more are handled through these modules. Nevertheless, regardless of any complex applications, any real-time system at the architectural level can be represented with these four modules.

Product Model

Since we picked up a very simple design example, the input and output processing modules don't act much on the signals other than simple scaling and range checks. Therefore the heavy load would fall on the Control and Monitor modules. As we discussed, before and after performing PBS, we created four submodules as the following. Please note that, based on our requirement model these submodules are also divided to be based on two different subfunctions, data and control, DFD0, and CFD0. Please see Figure 8-3 for details.

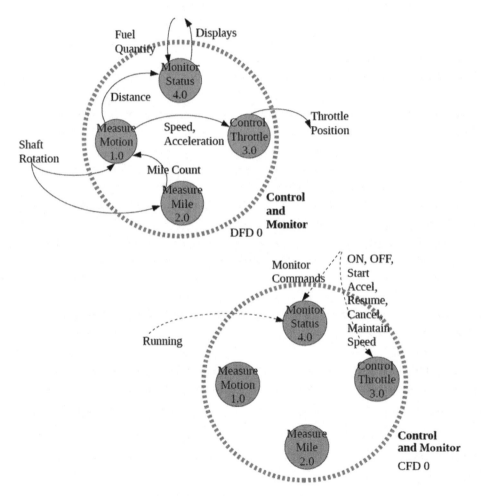

Figure 8-3. *A reminder of DFD and CFD in the order to be converted to their equivalent models in MBD*

As is evident from the requirements models, the number or the nature of the inputs and outputs of the Control and Monitor modules do not change as we proceed to the lower layers of design, they just become more defined and consequently assigned to various submodules for further processing. In Figure 8-4, the MBD version of the Control and Monitor module is being represented. The number and nature of all inputs and outputs is being projected from the higher level of the requirements model. As we decomposed the higher module to four different submodules, we might create more data and control signals. As a result we can combine or decompose the data and control buses to fewer or more signals and buses respectively. In this case we decided not to combine the local signals with the global signals for the memory space considerations.

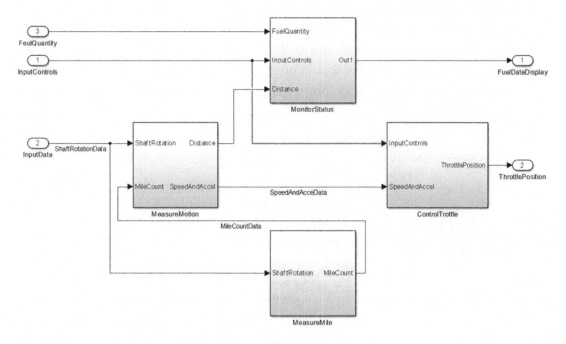

Figure 8-4. *An equivalent CFD and DFD in MDB*

In addition to the data bus, we decomposed the input control signal to two signals for the ease of use and the application requirement. These techniques can be used throughout the development process and will be considered as activities under Process Model development. As we discussed before the process model deals with architectural concerns, V&V, optimizations, and process design. Again, the MBD model represents the requirements model in a one-to-one fashion. In the following paragraphs we follow the same trends in the requirements model until we get to the PSPEC and CPSEC documents.

Further decomposing the product, we have decided that the modules, Measure Motion 1.0 and Measure Mile 2.0, are simple enough that they won't need further decomposition. The remaining modules are Control Throttle 3.0 and Monitor Status 4.0 modules that seem to be complex enough to need to be broken down into detailed submodules. On a side note, when a module appears not to need additional decomposition, therefore by definition the module is called a component. As a reminder, components are the simplest building blocks of the product that can be designed and tested in one sprint (Task-Component). The followings are the requirements model Control Throttle module that will follow with the MBD equivalent model.

In accordance with the requirements model for this level of the product, the Control Throttle module is decomposed to three submodules: Select Speed 3.1, Maintain Speed 3.2, and Maintain Accel 3.3. Again, the data and control models are presented in separate representations. However, due to MBD tools shortcomings, there is no separate representation for each; rather we should organize the MBD model in a way that control signals are separate from their data counterparts. Please see Figure 8-5.

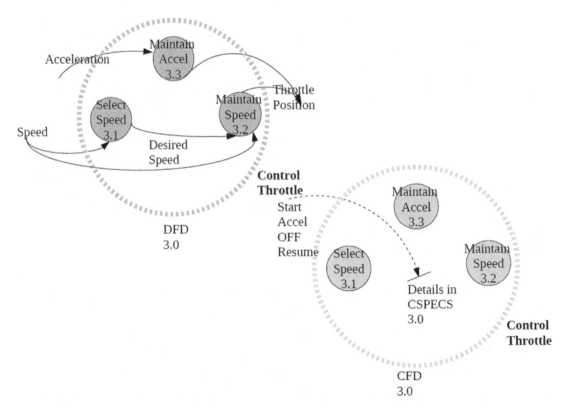

Figure 8-5. The CFD and DFD modules to be converted to MBD

As we can see in Figure 8-6 of the MBD model, it shows how the InputControls control signal can interact with the data selection. Depending on what the value of InputControls is, either we maintain a constant acceleration or we disregard any acceleration and continue with the zero acceleration, which is also the constant speed. The vertical dark bar on the left side denotes a bus selector in Simulink for selecting and routing signals whether it is of a data or control nature. The vertical dark bar on the right side is a bus creator that would multiplex signals regardless of their nature. In our process we don't mix and match data signals with control signals. This is the only way to overcome the MBD tools shortcomings to allow the users to create separate data and control layers.

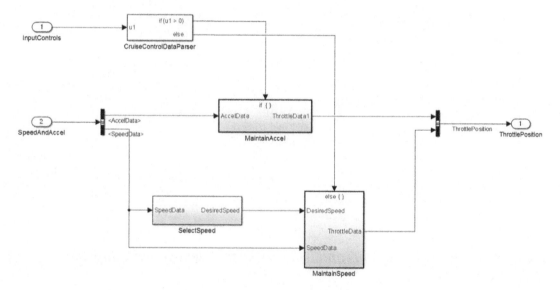

Figure 8-6. *An equivalent MBD of the previous CFD and DFD*

We continue our journey on the same level to develop the Monitor Status module. This module comprises of two submodules, Monitor Fuel Consumption and Monitor Average Speed. By inspecting the requirements model we realized there are three inputs to the module and one display output. Two of the inputs are of a data nature and the one remaining is of a control nature. Since Running is one of the EngineStatus conditions it is of a control nature. As we have remembered the InputControls bus contains both EngineStatus and CruiseControl signals. StartTrip and AverageSpeedRequest are part of the CruiseControl control signals (Figure 8-7).

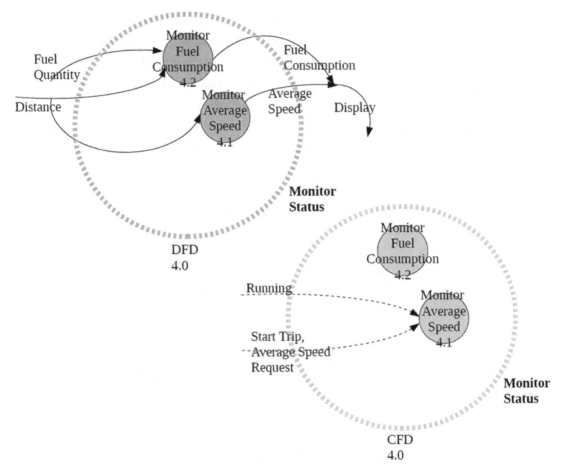

Figure 8-7. *The last set of CFD and DFD on the first tier of architecture to be converted to MBD*

Figure 8-8 represents the MBD model for the Figure 8-7 requirements model. As we expected, the relationship between modules, inputs, and outputs are one to one. The average speed and Fuel Consumption are the result of the process and they are out to be displayed to the driver.

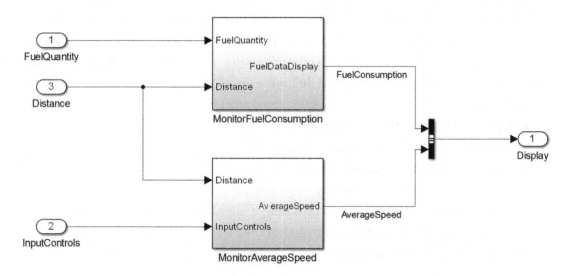

Figure 8-8. *The equivalent model in MBD*

Since the module Monitor Fuel Consumption has reached its simplest form, it is now considered to be a component. However this is not true for the other module at the same PBS level, Monitor Average Speed. Figure 8-9 is the PBS of this module, which is comprised of three different components: Start Trip Time, Clock Trip Time, and Issue Average Speed.

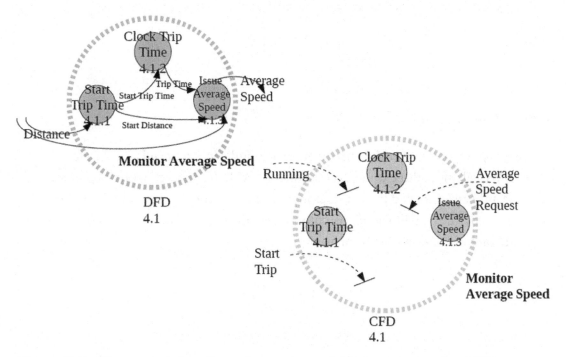

Figure 8-9. *The second tier of requirements model to be converted to MBD*

At this point, we can design our data layer with the help of the above DFD 4.1 but we need more info to be able to design the CFD4.1 in conjunction with the DFD4.1. The interdependency of these two data and control entities are needed. As a result we define the following for the CFD4.1. Since this definition concludes our control layer we will call it the CSPEC:

CSPEC 4.1: Monitor Average Speed

Start Trip Time will activate process 4.1.1

Running will activate process 4.1.2

Average Speed Request will activate process 4.1.3

With these new definitions we can now design our MBD model. The control arrows on top of each module are trigger points that would be activated if their corresponding conditions are met. Please see Figure 8-10.

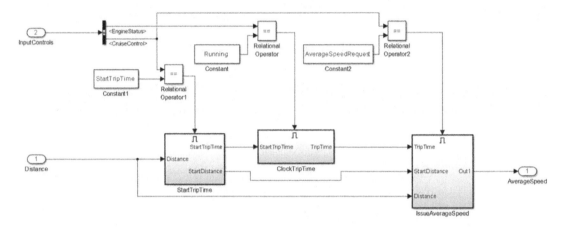

Figure 8-10. *The equivalent MBD*

At this point our last module has been successfully decomposed to its last layer of DFD. We call these three units as components. With the exception of component CSPEC4.1 that was needed to be implemented a layer higher before other components were reached, we can address all the components throughout the project at the same time and on the same architectural level.

For the Measure Motion component we have the following function definition:

PSPEC 1.0: Measure Motion

```
Distance_Count ++;
Distance = Distance_Count/Mile_Count;
Speed = Pulse_Rate/Mile_Count;
Accel = Rate_Change/Mile_Count;
```

In the MBD environment this will translate to the following executable model in Figure 8-11.

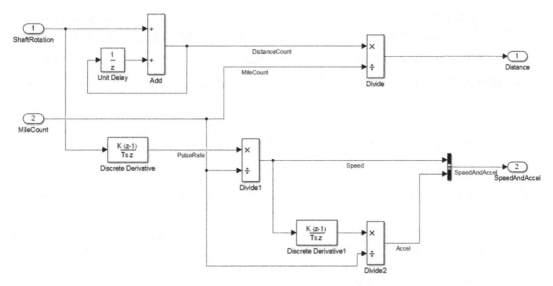

Figure 8-11. *The equivalent MBD for PSPEC 1.0*

Since the inputs and outputs of the component were already defined, the function definition was easy to implement. This also would streamline the workload for the development engineers, thus speeding up the development process. The next step would be to develop the Measure Mile functionality. Although the functionality of Measure Mile component precedes the Measure Motion component, it has no effect on the development process as a whole. This makes task distribution easy for the project architect leading to overlapping tasks and saving even more time. Below is the function definition of the Measure Mile component in requirements model form:

PSPEC 2.0: Measure Mile

```
Shaft_Rotation_Pulse += ;
Calculate_Pulse_Count (Shaft_Rotation_Pulse);
If Lower_Limit<= Shaft_Rotation_Pulse <=Upper_Limit
        set Mile_Count = Shaft_Rotation_Pulse;
Otherwise
        set Mile_Count = Default_Mile_Count;
```

Figure 8-12 is the representation of the above pseudo-code in MBD language. There are various ways to implement conditional statements via MBD tools, and they are all the right way based on the developer's style in programming. Try to have an open mind with the programming styles.

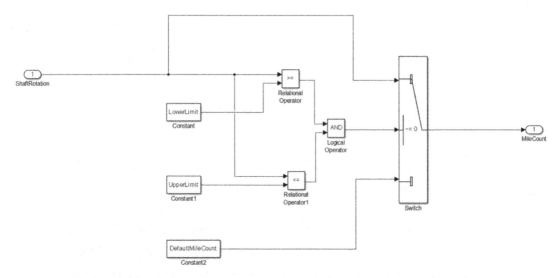

Figure 8-12. *MBD model for PSPEC 2.0*

The CSPEC3.0 is described rather in a finite state machine fashion. This method of expressing requirements is exactly translatable to a MBD model. However we found a simpler way to express the requirement for control and data all in one place. This part was also implemented when the Control Throttle PSEPC was implemented. The remaining PSPEC and CSPECs can be easily defined based on the same method we have demonstrated so far.

The main advantage of utilizing an MBD tool is that at the end of the process of defining the requirements, you have also designed and implemented the product functionalities and features. In addition, you have the option of simulating the results before implementing the design on real hardware. This will save a tremendous amount of work and prevent a massive amount of waste.

Next we will revisit what we've learned about the process and product model through studying the requirements model in the light of MBD.

MBD and Process Model

The process model covers a host of different and often complex activities that might seem related or even not directly related to the product development. Timing Specifications, Requirement Dictionary, Operating Systems, Database Architecture, DCD & CCD, Optimization, V&V(MBD Model Testing, Product Bench Testing, Smoke Test), Continuous Integration, Manufacturing Process (Functional Test, End-of-the-Line Test), and the Deployment (product optimization, troubleshooting, and diagnostics) are just some of them.

In Agile and DFM processes all these activities are part of what is called the product infant care period. This shows that the development process continues even after the product is released for at least a few months or years. This is why there should be a uniform method and tool that can connect all these activities like a thread that holds together a series of beads. Fortunately, MBD tools have the capability to properly connect all these activities. However, the MBD environment as a tool is only capable of providing the means to materialize your concept but are not able to show you the road map of how to organize, design, and implement these activities in order to create a uniform development process from research to manufacturing. Yet, if you are utilizing MBD tools, the requirements model can be implemented much easier and that will provide you the road map you are looking for to carry your product from concept through manufacturing and beyond.

One of the most important things that a road map is able to provide you with is a prioritization task list. If you let the product speak to you, then function with higher rates of executions, or in other words, high-frequency functions take the higher priority over lower-frequency functions. This is because in real-time systems the critical tasks execute on a more frequent basis than the others. These functions contain the core functionality of the product. To make a list of these functions based on their priority ranking, you need to develop your timing specifications. The development of timing specs is on a layers basis because as you remember you are developing your product based on PBS and the top-down approach. Do not worry about reshuffling the functions around as the design constraints kick in. With MBD this would be much easier than what you think.

Timing Specifications

As you might remember from the requirement models, we asked you not to worry about the timing specification of the product functions while you are developing the product models on each layer. This was for when the requirements model was executed at on phase-gate basis. Once you move to the realm of MBD then you can take advantage of early V&V processes while you are developing your product as early as the concept phase with all the in-the-loop methods. In MIL at concept, you don't need timing specs because you can run all the functions at the same time. This is when you are testing your algorithms. Once you moved to the SIL and HIL stages then you can start worrying about assigning execution time to each module. The software timing requirement is a constraint that the real world imposes on the product. This is because during SIL and HIL testing, the computation power of your microprocessors and the valuable resource of time are not limitless. In an ideal world, while doing MIL, all functions in a real-time system can be executed simultaneously, but that's not always possible. This is when we create Interrupt Service Routines that run with different frequencies and priorities. So the rule of thumb is to run your algorithms in an ideal and pure simulation environment.

In the meantime we don't want to impose the timing constraints at the beginning of the design process because this would sidetrack our brainstorming process and would impose unrealistic restrictions on the product functions and features, often creating unreliable test results for your algorithms. Assign execution time when you have benchmarked your algorithms in an ideal environment. You never know, as the timing spec is a fluid concept and often changes as we learn more about our product and its applications. This concept is also evident in CPM when the project manager starts to define the project tasks and activities. The rule of thumb is to apply constraints after the concept is developed. For this very reason, the requirements model also asks you to define the timing specifications at the end when all the product modules and components at least on the same layer are defined. For our example of automobile cruise control, we developed the Figure 8-13 timing specification from the CSPEC of the core cruise control module.

Input	Event	Output	Event	Response Time
ON	Turns on	Throttle Position	Goes to idle state	0.5 sec max
Resume	Turns on	Throttle Position	Goes to cruising state	0.5 sec max
OFF	Turns off	Throttle Position	Goes to inactive state	0.5 sec max
Start Accel	Turns on	Throttle Position	Goes to Accelerating state	0.5 sec max
Maintain Accel	Turns on	Throttle Position	Goes to Accelerating state	0.5 sec max
Running	Turns on	Throttle Position	Goes to Monitor Average Speed	0.5 sec max
Shaft Rotation	Rotation Rate Changes	Throttle Position	To Cruising, Displayed	1 sec max
Fuel Quantity	Entered	Fuel Consumption	Displayed	10 sec max
Avg Spd Rqst	Turns on	Avg Spd	Displayed	1 sec max
Start Trip	-	-	-	No time-critical output
Start Msrd Mile	-	-	-	

Figure 8-13. *Timing specification table for cruise control module*

After analyzing the table and realizing it is inefficient to have individual timing requirements for each component, also for the sake of this example, we decided to group the similar functionalities together based on the architectural template. The system inputs and outputs plus the main computational module will run at the fastest speed and the noncritical user interface data will run at the slowest rate. You can also at this stage rehash the architectural layout and move the components and modules from one speed bracket to another or mix and match various function speeds to lower or higher depending on the applications. We decided to do Figure 8-14 for our example here.

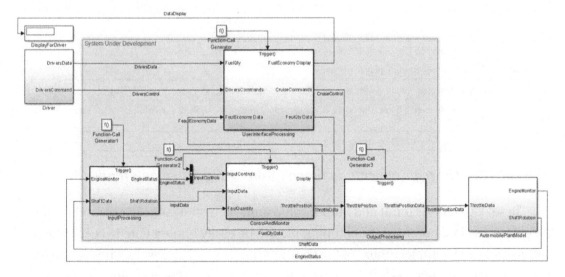

Figure 8-14. *The timing spec integrated into the top level model*

So as you see, we weren't worried about our timing until we go to the CSPEC level and then we allowed the application to dictate the timing spec to the product. The timing spec then was applied to the top layer. The function calls in Figure 8-14 can be triggered at a certain point in time independent from each other with adjustable frequency. The MBD limitation here would be to create asynchronous and preemptive interrupt schemes. However each function call can be packaged neatly and manually placed in the right Interrupt service routine.

Now if the plant model is a dynamic model, then we can dynamically simulate the model before deploying it on a real hardware or we can do a host of different methods such as MIL, SIL, and HIL. I can't put enough emphasis on simulation before I am being accused of prejudice against traditional methods. The simulation will significantly reduce the time to market of the product not at the design stage but at the troubleshooting, optimization, and deployment phases. The data collected from the system can also be used for troubleshooting and diagnostics efforts in the field. This data works as a product signature for benchmarking purposes.

Requirements Dictionary

Figure 8-15 is a simplified requirements dictionary for our example.

Definitions, States, Units	Data/Control
Accel = Measure Vehicle Acceleration\Units: Miles per hour per sec.	D
Activate = Driver's cruise control activation command\ Two values: ON, OFF.	C
Avg Spd = Calculated Average Trip Speed\ Units: Miles per hour.	D
Avg Spd Rqst = Driver's request to display the average speed.	C
Cruise Commands = Maintain Speed, Select Speed, Start Accel, Maintain Accel, Resume, ON, OFF, Cancel.	C
Shaft Rotation = Input pulse stream corresponding to angular rotation of drive shaft\ Units:Arbitrary angular unit per pulse.	D
Fuel Quantity = Entered value of fill-up fuel quantity\ Units: Gallons	D

Figure 8-15. *The requirements dictionary from the requirements model*

These data such as input and output value units along the range of acceptable values for each input and output of the components can be easily implemented via executable scripts and can be implemented in the code automatically. The absolute min and max values are vital to many system inputs as the digital world has its own limitations. For example, a divide by zero can result in a catastrophic system failure. These MBD scripts can not only document the knowledge, but they can also help you to implement a bounded input, bounce output (BIBO) control scheme.

Real-Time Operating Systems

It is impossible to talk about timing specification for a real-time system without mentioning real-time operating systems. In a digital control system the sampling time is an integral part of every routine. The sampling time in a real-time system technically translates to the frequency of interrupts that call those specific routines. Since time is a scarce resource not all routines can run at the same time or with the same frequency. That's why we go a long way to identify which routines are absolutely critical and which are not. This is when the application of hard and soft real-time routines can make a difference in how a critical application differs from a noncritical one.

Depending on the memory availability, the routines can be categorized as either processes or threads. Processes use separate memory locations where threads use the same memory locations. High integrity applications usually use processes and threads are for lightweight, noncritical applications or background tasks. Processes can then be categorized to hard deadline, soft deadline, periodic, and aperiodic processes. This is where the real-time operating systems comes to play hard. Real-time operating systems are to manage processes and threads through various means and methods. Discussing operating systems in detail is beyond the scope of this book but we will discuss how some of the MBD tools have integrated operating systems into their toolboxes. The morale of the story is that, assigning execution frequency to each module is not enough. We also have to manage the timing specifications via operating systems that would oversee not only the software but also hardware and the entire system's architecture.

Mathworks Simulink environment in conjunction with the Texas Instrument DSP/BIOS operating system have created a MBD feature that allow integrating the operating system of the TI microprocessors into the Simulink models. This feature uses almost every object and tools that the TI DSP/BIOS offers without requiring you to hand-code the OS. You can create and embed, hardware interrupts (HWI), software interrupt (SWI), and many other software objects.

Database Architecture

Similar to operating systems, databases are also complicated and come with various architectures. Discussing this topic is also far beyond the scope of this book, but after, all with the timing specifications comes the operating systems and with operating systems there you must use some types of databases to handle data among processes and threads that run at different speeds. This is very important especially for the critical processes not to be starved of their data. Some processes need the most accurate data and some need the most recent data and some need both. For the most recent data processes the example that comes to mind is LIFO buffers where the first data reading in the stack is the last data out, which means the most recent data is always retrieved from the stack. For the most accurate data we can bring an example from moving average filters where a series of data will be averaged out and the most accurate estimate would be provided to the consumer of the data. In motor control application, the current value read off the motor windings should be the most accurate and recent data. Just as an example for databases, one of the most popular database structures used in real-time system architecture is called the Producer-Consumer model. Figure 8-16 is a model created in the National Instrument LabView environment. The main idea here is that, the producer and consumer routines are running at different speeds; however there is a buffer in between that would allow for a reliable data exchange between these two entities.

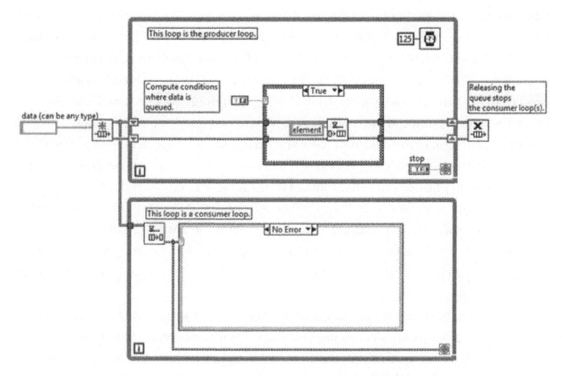

Figure 8-16. *Database schema implementation in NI LabView*

When it comes to data handling, electrical or computer engineers have no say. This is the domain for software engineers who can remedy various situations with their tools and methods. Layers models make the interaction between these two very different engineering disciplines much smoother. It will actively involve the software engineers in the process of developing the architecture of a real-time system.

The level of involvement of software engineers is more visible at the beginning of the development as they lead the module structures; however they will continue supporting the developers throughout the process in order to organize and manage the data, define architectures, and set up an effective operating system that looks beyond the product function into manufacturing, deployment, and field service.

Verification and Validation (V&V)

One of the tools that often comes with MBD software is used for automated requirement tracing, standard compliance checking, and the coverage analysis. Some of them also can create automated test harnesses for each model to check model functionality, testing against the requirements and model coverage. Figure 8-17 is an example of Mathworks

Simulink V&V toolbox. For the highly regulated industries such as medical, defense, and aviation, these documents are required by the government and are vital to the life of the development in order to acquire appropriate certifications. Since the majority of these documents are created automatically at the time that models are created, it is a good practice to perform the V&V processes right after the models are developed whether or not the norm of your industry requires them. This way the design flaws will be identified earlier on in the design process and can be resolved much quickly and easily than later. Postponing the V&V process will push the design bugs to the intergeneration and deployment phases, where the product is much more complex and debugging takes longer time to carry out and bugs will be much more expensive to fix. Some small software to hardware bugs can delay or even kill the product. Another advantage of utilizing MBD's V&V tools is that the requirement specification, design, V&V, and later optimization can be performed one after another, leaving less workload on the shoulders of the integration process.

Please note that there are examples on the Mathworks website that illiterate how requirements specs are created via the Doors application, where the requirement statements are created and stored. Doors software looks a lot like MS Excel but it can capture the marketing definition of the product in hierarchical and cascaded style much or less similar to our requirements model. Also the automatically generated code is embedded in the requirements model definition as comments in the body of the code. This is required with some agencies for traceability purposes, creating a one-to-one relationship between requirements items and their counterpart design MBD model with the automated test harness created by the Simulink according to the requirement specifications and design. Again, this stage is also required for traceability but aside from the government enforcement, it is a very useful method of debugging the design. Creating test cases for each model will allow the designer to explore the design in a way that it was not possible before, allowing them to create complex test situations to study the functionality of design under different circumstances. Additionally, in the Simulink environment you can create test cases for each requirement item. This is how to demonstrate that each test harness is testing the design, item by item. Finally Simulink can provide you with coverage test results that would test the design against common flaws, such as the following: if the bounded input creates a bounded output, whether the module outputs are going to converge or diverge, if there are dead logics used, and so on. These and a handful of other reports can create a concrete V&V process with a host of useful documents, all generated automatically.

Continuous Integration

In an MBD environment, the automated code generation and continuous integration can be combined. Obviously the entire process can be automated and performed without any interruption as the configuration parameters of the automated code generation process can be fully programmed and controlled. The generated code from the model can then be automatically inserted into the hand-coded system programs, creating homogeneous code. As the code is generated from the models, the code can be automatically passed on to the next process, the smoke test. The last stage of development is the smoke test, which marks the end of continuous integration process. These process-from-design to integration and smoke tests all can happen in one Scrum's Sprint.

Smoke Test

If you remember, we talked about creating test cases for each MBD model. The component test cases have different natures as the higher-level integration model tests. Architecting the development tests from component to integration can fill up a few book volumes. As in the manufacturing processes, the subassembly's functional testing is different than the end-of-line testing of the complete product; the component testing is normally much more detailed where the integration testing is more streamlined, leaving studying the details of a component's function to the more detailed component tests.

The smoke test is also an integration test but with the difference that the test is being performed on the latest version of our final product, not just the software. Having an eye on the integration and smoke testing while we are designing our functional modules and components, we can create a systematic method to extract integration test cases from the component test cases. In other words, the integration test is the collection of the best detailed test cases at the component level. If we decide to have an integration model for our MBD models, these test cases can be used to simulate the integration model, which is a tremendous help with troubleshooting as the architecture gets more crowded and complicated. The integration model is the equivalent architectural model of the requirement model for our product. Finally an abstract of the integration model's test cases can be utilized in the smoke test, and then these test cases are transferred to the manufacturing for product testing.

Manufacturing Tests

Manufacturing tests are nothing but the subsets of component and integration models test cases. As we discussed before, the manufacturing tests have two distinct styles with respect to product functionality coverage. The subassembly functional tests are compared to module test cases and the end-of-the-line tests are similar to integration and smoke tests.

The test plans and codes generated in the development process can accordingly be used in the manufacturing process with zero to minimal changes. The industry leaders use the actual module test cases for the manufacturing tests. By doing so, they eliminate the need for introducing other sets of software packages along expertise with different skill sets. For example, if you are using MBD to develop your product software and then you are using C language to develop your manufacturing test routines, then you will need separate hardware platforms compatible to MBD and C, respectively, in addition to hiring programmers with special domain expertise to develop these codes. Keep in mind, you also need to maintain two different development systems. Otherwise by using only one development tool across the board, the tool can be utilized throughout the development and manufacturing process. By unifying the tools for the two major players of the development, design, and manufacturing, the rest of development will follow. Diagnostics aside from promoting user friendliness for your product creates a major source of income in form of service that also buys you customer loyalty, which consequently gives you an unprecedented advantage over your competitors.

Diagnostics

Among all product testing processes you do to ensure the integrity of product quality and function, diagnostics is the most complex and most useful one to the customers. This product feature makes a tremendous differentiating factor between you and your competitors. However, many products fail to offer such a hugely beneficial feature to their users despite the fact your product developers have already done most of the work for it without knowing it. The diagnostics is a subset of developmental process with respect to component and module testing. The developer engineers as a part of their routine processes create benchmarks and methods to distinguish a good functional performance against a faulty one. If these efforts are abstracted, organized, and offered to the customer through a user-friendly interface, they are what the customer likes to use to find out if the product is functioning properly or there are signs of wear and tear that can cause failures in the future.

The diagnostics algorithms can either be extracted directly from the MBD models and offered in their native style to the customers through plug-in packages, and/or they can be packaged and sold separately as diagnostics and monitoring tools. If you use plug-in packages of product software, then you can activate and deactivate the diagnostics layer by some digital keys.

Summary

As we demonstrated in this chapter, the MBD tools can be utilized throughout the development process from very early stages of product inception until it's released to the customers and even after the release. Historically, most MBD tools were originated to help the research engineers to materialize their ideas and concepts. As the tools structurally and architecturally evolved and were equipped with more features intended to help the design engineers with their needs, their evolutionary process didn't stop at design. Modern MBD tools, as they are evolving, tare growing toward system integration and product deployment.

The MBD tools have provided us with powerful means that enable us to unify the language of experts involved in design and manufacturing of the real-time systems. Utilizing one development tool can eliminate distractions in the development process, allowing the engineers to focus more on product development rather than developing skill sets for different tools. This also eliminates the tools' compatibility issues, reduces the risk of tools' early obsolescence, and simplifies the tools' maintenance programs resulting in much lower development costs.

Additionally, by removing the tool variation in the development process and eliminating unnecessary interfaces between phases of product development from concept to requirement, to design, to implementation, to test, to manufacturing, we shorten the time to market of the product via two methods, removing unnecessary utility work such as codes and hardware that translate the output of one development phase to the input of another one. It also facilitates the product development by unifying the technical languages and methods, which in return will save time in understanding the product and development issues regardless of their geographical differences.

Finally, the tools are dumb. Only a well-thought-out process gets the best of your tools. This process needs an active architecture. The layers model is able to provide your development process a structure flexible enough that can welcome changes while ensuring the integrity of the product functions.

Index

A

Agile methods
  meaning, 37
  overview, 36
  principals, 58
  project control
    burn-down/up charts, 41
    cone of uncertainty, 41
    cost, quality, time and scope, 40
    daily stand-ups, 39
    design phase, 42
    done-done list, 39
    interfaces, tools and methods, 39
    potentially shippable product, 39
    pyramid, 40
    release planning, 42
    sprint, 40
    team members, 39
  Scrum, 37
    rooming, 38
    master, 37
    sprint planning, 38
Analog to digital converter hardware
  (ADC), 67
Architectural drawing, 12
  building construction, 24
  construction engineers, 21
  cross-sectional view, 20–21
  first floor, 16
  flow structure, 13
  front and east elevation, 18
  garage floor, 15
  layer creation, 22
  numbering system, 23
  reusability, maintainability, readability
    and scalability, 22
  second floor, 17
  stack of, 23
  west and rear elevation, 19
Architectural model, 139

B

Building industry *vs.* PCBs, 24

C

Collaborative product development
  (CPD), 43
  concept development, 44
  design, 45
  financial tool, 43
  gate one, 44
  gate two, 45
  manufacturing, 46
  phases, 43
  product launch, 46
  product planning/project and
    architecture, 45
  project completion, 47
  software process, 52
  tasks, deliverables
    and decisions, 44
  testing, 46
  V&V and optimization, 46

Conceptual design
    product development, 76
    prototypes, 75
    rapid prototyping
        hardware in the loop, 79
        model in the loop, 77
        proof of concept, 81
        software in the loop, 78
    Scrum concept, 75
    simulation prototyping, 76
Context diagram, 92
    abstract document, 92
    architectural units, 94
    control flow diagrams, 92
    customer's view, 92
    DCD and CCD
        comparison, 94
    embedded system, 92–93
    HP's method, 93
    submodules, 94
Continuous integration (CI)
    process model, MBD, 203
    software environment, 106
Control Flow Diagram (CFD), 95
Control specifications (CPSEC)
    MBD tools, 122
    problem statement, 135
Critical path methods (CPM), 28
    definition, 29
    effectiveness of, 29
    Robust Gantt Chart, 29
    WBS, 30

D

Data context and control context diagrams
    (DCD and CCD), 127
    control and monitor system, 127

electronics control module, 127
    graph, 127, 128
Data flow and control flow diagrams
    (DFD and CFD), 129
    complex module and control throttle, 131
    components, 129
    data and control structures, 133–134
    module, control and monitor, 129–130
    monitor status module, 132
Data flow diagram (DFD), 95
Design for manufacturing (DFM), 54

E, F, G

Electronics control module (ECM), 127
Embedded systems, 7

H, I, J, K

Hardware interrupts (HWI), 199
Hardware in the loop (HIL), 79
Hatley and Pirbhai (HP) method
    process architecture, 143
    progressive product test, 107
    requirement model, 91, 101
Highly accelerated life testing (HALT), 52

L

Land survey drawings, 10
Layers architecture
    Agile methods, 3
    bottlenecks, 8
    building industry *vs*. PCBs, 24
    clash of
        cultures, 5
        thoughts, 5
    construction industry, 9

construction project, 1
control functions, 3
draw (*see* Architectural drawing)
efficient development method, 2
embedded systems, 1, 7
firmware, 7
green process, 2
history of, 5
intelligent product development, 8
land survey drawings, 10
mission creation, 4
people and product development, 6
project manager, 3
projects and processes, 6
requirement model, 4
software and hardware, 4
software development, 7
Layers model. *See* Model-based
    design (MBD)

M, N, O

Management process and architectural
    tool, 61
    architecture design, 82
    classical method, 61
    documentation process, 63
    phase (*see* Requirement model)
    requirement model, 62
    software and hardware, 62
    traditional methods, 61
    vehicle cruise control, 82
Marketing requirements document
    (MRD), 74, 91
Model-based design (MBD), 163
    architecture, 176
    behavioral model, 178
    build process, 177

control and data, 85
layers model, 174, 179
in-the-loop solutions, 175
model creation, 164
platforms, 181
product and process, 164
    architectural layers, 168
    control algorithms, 165
    development model, 169
    embedded systems, 166
    manufacturing processes, 172
    MBD model, 166
    modeling languages, 56
    process model, 166
    product development, 171
    product's process model, 166
    rapid prototyping, 77
    Simulink environment, 167
    SST product, 165
rapid prototyping, 173
requirements model, 183
    architecture and specifications, 185
    overview, 184
    process model, 195
    product model, 186
tools, 172
UML program, 163
utilization steps, 173
Model in the loop (MIL)
    hardware loop, 77
    software loop, 78

P, Q

Polaris defense system, 29
Problem statement
    automobile management system, 125
    control and monitor unit, 126

Problem statement (*cont.*)
    control diagram, 126
    requirements model, 126
        architectural model, 139
        DCD and CCD, 127
        DFD and CFD, 129
        PSPECs and CSPECs, 135
        timing specification, 137
    system architecture, 140
    understand, 125
Process architecture
    Agile testing, 160
    design and planning project, 153
        development process, 153–154
        hardware, 154
        method recycling, 155
        software, 154
        system architecture, 153
        team dynamics, 155
    final phases
        Agile development
          process, 158–159
        layer architecture, 158
        phase-gate concept, 157
        structured Scrum framework, 157
    HP method, 143
    inspiration, 145
    modules and components, 155
    POC (*see* Proof of Concept (POC))
    potentially shippable product
        concept, 144
    smoke test, 159
    V-Model structure, 144
Process model, MBD, 195
    continuous integration, 203
    database architecture, 200
    diagnostics, 204
    frequency functions, 195
    manufacturing tests, 204
    product infant care, 195
    real-time operating systems, 199
    requirements dictionary, 198
    smoke test, 203
    timing specifications, 196
        brainstorming process, 196
        cruise control module, 197
        dynamic model, 198
        functions, 196
        top level model, 197
    verification and validation, 201
Process specification (PSPEC)
    MBD tools, 122
    problem statement, 135
Product breakdown structure (PBS)
    component design, 86
    data layer, 116
    development, 114
    DFD and CFD interact, 114
    hardware and software platforms, 68–69
Product development team, 69
Product life cycle, 67
Product model, MBD, 186
    control and monitor module, 187
    data counterparts, 188
    definition concludes, 192
    DFD and CFD models, 186
    equivalent model, 191, 192
    executable model, 193
    first tier architecture, 190
    function definition, 193
    measure mile component, 194
    representation, 194
    second tier, 191
Project management methods
    Agile methods, 36, 58
    collaborative product development, 43

CPM (*see* Critical path methods (CPM))

design for manufacturing, 54

documentation process, 57

interfaces, 59

modeling languages, 56

optimization, 57

pyramid, 36

real-time system, 27

Scrum functions, 57

software, 47

time-critical and predictable basis, 28

V-Model, 58

Proof of concept (POC), 81

architectural development, 146

conceptualization phase, 146

CPD phases, 145

forms and engineering methods, 146

hardware recycle, 147

logical process, 145

method recycling, 148

prototypes, 146

Scrum practitioners

concept phases, 150

concept release, 150

DFM, 151

prototyping phase, 151

scaled control diagram, 152

software recycle, 148

team dynamics, 148

concept development and manufacturing, 149

marketing and research engineering role, 150

purchasing department, 149

V-Model, 146

R

Real-time operating systems, 199

Requirement model

Agile methodologies, 64

architectural template

development process, 64

functional modules, 65–66

hardware/software modules and interfaces, 66

reusability section, 64

system architecture, 65

user-interface processing, 66

communication theory

control firmware, 71

functional requirements, 73

interfaces, 70

internal and external customers, 71

system architecture, 71

temperature compensation, 73

temperature sensitivity, 71

V-Model and CPD frameworks, 71

conceptual design (*see* Conceptual design)

consequential requirements, 92

context diagrams, 92

control and process specifications, 103

creation, 70

design and review process, 102

development team, 69

dictionary, 99

flow diagrams

DFD and CFD representations, 95–96

top-down view, 95, 97

HP method, 101

inputs, outputs and functions, 63

inspect and adapt, 102

internal and external data, 102–103

marketing requirements document, 74

Requirement model (*cont.*)
 modeling tools, 103
 module design, 83
  constitutes, 85
  data and control layers, 84
  MBD control modules, 85
  super-modules constitute, 83
  time-series representation, 86
 PBS components, 86
 product breakdown structure, 68
 product life cycle, 67
 process and controls, 91
 PSPEC, CSPEC specification, 97
 Scrum, 63 (*see also* Scrum structure)
 time-consuming practice, 102
 timing specifications, 100
Robust Gantt Chart, 29

S

Scaled Agile Framework (SAF), 170
Scrum structure
 Agile process, 104
 CPD/V-Model life cycle, 120
 design approach
  architectural layer, 116
  functional hierarchy, 116–117
  PBS approach, 118
 external data process, 118
 integrating layers model, 121
 MBD tools, 122
 PBS development, 114
 pragmatic method, 104
 project management, 104
 robust, 104
 V-Model (*see* V-Model)
Smoke test, 159
Software interrupt (SWI), 199

Software in the loop (SIL), 78
Software project
  management, 47
 CPD process, 52
 development process, 49
 drivers, 48
 embedded system, 49
 layers, 47
 maintainability, 51
 readability, 51
 reusability and scalability, 51
 V-Model, 53
Solid state transformer (SST), 165

T

Timing specifications, 100

U

Unified modeling language (UML), 56
Unit Under Test (UUT), 78

V

Verification and Validation (V&V), 201
V-Model, 104
 component level, 106
 continuous integration, 106
 CPM method, 53
 design branch, 53
 flat
  modification, 109
  omitted concept and release
   phases, 109
  Scrum framework, 110
 hardware and software
  platform, 106

highly document oriented, 53
implementation, 50, 58
parallel phases, 54
product development
    Agile friendly process, 111
    core processing unit, 111
    engineering functions, 113
    identification of, 112
    life cycle, 113
    potentially shippable
      product, 111
    product test phase, 113
    system architecture, 111
    T-shape concept, 112
    visualization, 112
progressive product test
    End of Line testing, 107
    milestone testing, 108
    smoke test concept, 108
    testing process, 107
    validation tests, 107

requirements, design and
    implementation phases, 104
software development process, 54
software life cycle, 53
structured Scrum environment, 105

W, X, Y, Z

Work breakdown structures (WBS), 30
    constraints, 33
    decomposing processes, 30–31
    development process, 33
    direct contents, 32
    Gantt chart representation, 34
    product functions, 30
    project and product developments, 30
    project control, 35
    project scope, 31
    resource planning, 35
    scopes and deliverables, 32
    task delegation, 30

Get the eBook for only $5!

Why limit yourself?

With most of our titles available in both PDF and ePUB format, you can access your content wherever and however you wish—on your PC, phone, tablet, or reader.

Since you've purchased this print book, we are happy to offer you the eBook for just $5.

To learn more, go to http://www.apress.com/companion or contact support@apress.com.

Apress®

Made in the USA
Columbia, SC
22 February 2020